Flash MX 200 Basic

Student Manual

Gavin

Gavin @ gavinm . com

THOMSON

COURSE TECHNOLOGY ™

Australia • Canada • Mexico • Singapore
Spain • United Kingdom • United States

www. w3 schools . com
www. flash kit . com

Flash MX 2004: Basic

VP and GM of Courseware:	Michael Springer
Series Product Managers:	Caryl Bahner-Guhin and Adam A. Wilcox
Developmental Editor:	Brandon Heffernan
Copyeditor:	Geraldine Martin
Keytester:	Bill Bateman
Series Designer:	Adam A. Wilcox
Cover Designer:	Steve Deschene

For more information contact:

Course Technology
25 Thomson Place
Boston, MA 02210

Or find us on the Web at: www.course.com

For permission to use material from this text or product, submit a request online at: www.thomsonrights.com

Any additional questions about permissions can be submitted by e-mail to: thomsonrights@thomson.com

Trademarks

Course ILT is a trademark of Course Technology.

Some of the product names and company names used in this book have been used for identification purposes only and may be trademarks or registered trademarks of their respective manufacturers and sellers.

Disclaimer

Course Technology reserves the right to revise this publication and make changes from time to time in its content without notice.

ISBN 0-619-20422-2

Printed in the United States of America

2 3 4 5 PM 06 05 04

Contents

Flash MX 2004: Basic

Introduction

After reading this introduction, you will know how to:

A Use Course Technology ILT manuals in general.

B Use prerequisites, a target student description, course objectives, and a skills inventory to properly set your expectations for the course.

C Re-key this course after class.

Topic A: About the manual

Course Technology ILT philosophy

Course Technology ILT manuals facilitate your learning by providing structured interaction with the software itself. While we provide text to explain difficult concepts, the hands-on activities are the focus of our courses. By paying close attention as your instructor leads you through these activities, you will learn the skills and concepts effectively.

We believe strongly in the instructor-led classroom. During class, focus on your instructor. Our manuals are designed and written to facilitate your interaction with your instructor, and not to call attention to manuals themselves.

We believe in the basic approach of setting expectations, delivering instruction, and providing summary and review afterwards. For this reason, lessons begin with objectives and end with summaries. We also provide overall course objectives and a course summary to provide both an introduction to and closure on the entire course.

Manual components

The manuals contain these major components:

- Table of contents
- Introduction
- Units
- Course summary
- Quick reference
- Index

Each element is described below.

Table of contents

The table of contents acts as a learning roadmap.

Introduction

The introduction contains information about our training philosophy and our manual components, features, and conventions. It contains target student, prerequisite, objective, and setup information for the specific course.

Units

Units are the largest structural component of the course content. A unit begins with a title page that lists objectives for each major subdivision, or topic, within the unit. Within each topic, conceptual and explanatory information alternates with hands-on activities. Units conclude with a summary comprising one paragraph for each topic, and an independent practice activity that gives you an opportunity to practice the skills you've learned.

The conceptual information takes the form of text paragraphs, exhibits, lists, and tables. The activities are structured in two columns, one telling you what to do, the other providing explanations, descriptions, and graphics.

Course summary

This section provides a text summary of the entire course. It is useful for providing closure at the end of the course. The course summary also indicates the next course in this series, if there is one, and lists additional resources you might find useful as you continue to learn about the software.

Quick reference

The quick reference is an at-a-glance job aid summarizing some of the more common features of the software.

Index

The index at the end of this manual makes it easy for you to find information about a particular software component, feature, or concept.

Manual conventions

We've tried to keep the number of elements and the types of formatting to a minimum in the manuals. This aids in clarity and makes the manuals more classically elegant looking. But there are some conventions and icons you should know about.

Convention	Description
Italic text	In conceptual text, indicates a new term or feature.
Bold text	In unit summaries, indicates a key term or concept. In an independent practice activity, indicates an explicit item that you select, choose, or type.
`Code font`	Indicates code or syntax.
`Longer strings of ▶ code will look ▶ like this.`	In the hands-on activities, any code that's too long to fit on a single line is divided into segments by one or more continuation characters (▶). This code should be entered as a continuous string of text.
Select **bold item**	In the left column of hands-on activities, bold sans-serif text indicates an explicit item that you select, choose, or type.
Keycaps like (↵ ENTER)	Indicate a key on the keyboard you must press.

Hands-on activities

The hands-on activities are the most important parts of our manuals. They are divided into two primary columns. The "Here's how" column gives short instructions to you about what to do. The "Here's why" column provides explanations, graphics, and clarifications. Here's a sample:

Do it!

A-1: Creating a commission formula

Here's how	Here's why
1 Open Sales	This is an oversimplified sales compensation worksheet. It shows sales totals, commissions, and incentives for five sales reps.
2 Observe the contents of cell F4	$$\boxed{\text{F4} \quad \blacktriangledown} \quad \boxed{=} \quad \boxed{\text{=E4*C\_Rate}}$$ The commission rate formulas use the name "C_Rate" instead of a value for the commission rate.

For these activities, we have provided a collection of data files designed to help you learn each skill in a real-world business context. As you work through the activities, you will modify and update these files. Of course, you might make a mistake and, therefore, want to re-key the activity starting from scratch. To make it easy to start over, you will rename each data file at the end of the first activity in which the file is modified. Our convention for renaming files is to add the word "My" to the beginning of the file name. In the above activity, for example, a file called "Sales" is being used for the first time. At the end of this activity, you would save the file as "My sales," thus leaving the "Sales" file unchanged. If you make a mistake, you can start over using the original "Sales" file.

In some activities, however, it may not be practical to rename the data file. If you want to retry one of these activities, ask your instructor for a fresh copy of the original data file.

Topic B: Setting your expectations

Properly setting your expectations is essential to your success. This topic will help you do that by providing:

- Prerequisites for this course
- A description of the target student at whom the course is aimed
- A list of the objectives for the course
- A skills assessment for the course

Course prerequisites

Before taking this course, you should be familiar with personal computers and the use of a keyboard and a mouse. Furthermore, this course assumes that you've completed the following course or have equivalent experience:

- *Windows XP: Basic*

Target student

The target student for this course should be comfortable using a personal computer and Microsoft Windows XP or later. You'll get the most out of this course if your goal is to use Flash MX 2004 as a tool to create Flash movies for delivery on the Web.

Course objectives

These overall course objectives will give you an idea about what to expect from the course. It is also possible that they will help you see that this course is not the right one for you. If you think you either lack the prerequisite knowledge or already know most of the subject matter to be covered, you should let your instructor know that you think you are misplaced in the class.

After completing this course, you will know how to:

- Start Flash MX 2004, explore the Flash interface, create a new Flash file, import and manipulate images, convert bitmaps to vector graphics, create shapes by using the Pencil and Pen tools, and draw lines by using the Line tool.
- Create shapes by using the Rectangle, Oval, Pen, and Pencil tools, create freeform shapes, select and edit shapes by using the Selection, Lasso, and Free Transform tools, copy, move, and delete shapes, and group objects.
- Apply stroke and fill colors to a shape by using the Paint Bucket, Ink Bottle, and Eyedropper tools, and create custom colors, swatches, and gradients.
- Use the Text tool to create and modify text blocks and apply basic styles, alias small text, adjust the spacing, kerning, margins, and indentation of text, and use text utilities such as Find and Replace and the Spell Checker.
- Create, merge, rearrange, delete, and modify layers, create layer folders, mask a layer, lock a layer, show and hide a layer, and create a guide layer.
- Create a basic text animation, create a frame-by-frame animation, use Onion Skin, create a shape tweened animation, use shape hints, create a motion tweened animation, use a motion guide, control the speed of a motion tween, and arrange and extend frames.
- Create and edit button symbols, and duplicate and swap a button.

Skills inventory

Use the following form to gauge your skill level entering the class. For each skill listed, rate your familiarity from 1 to 5, with five being the most familiar. *This is not a test.* Rather, it is intended to provide you with an idea of where you're starting from at the beginning of class. If you're wholly unfamiliar with all the skills, you might not be ready for the class. If you think you already understand all of the skills, you might need to move on to the next course in the series. In either case, you should let your instructor know as soon as possible.

Skill	1	2	3	4	5
Starting Flash and exploring the Flash interface					
Creating a new Flash file					
Importing and manipulating images					
Converting bitmap images to vector images					
Creating shapes by using the Pencil and Pen tools					
Drawing lines by using the Line tool					
Creating shapes by using the Rectangle and Oval tools					
Selecting and editing shapes by using the Selection, Lasso, and Free Transform tools					
Applying stroke and fill colors to a shape by using the Paint Bucket, Ink Bottle, and Eyedropper tools					
Creating custom colors, swatches, and gradients					
Using the Text tool to create extending and fixed text blocks					
Formatting text					
Using the Find and Replace feature					
Using the Spell Checker feature					
Using the History panel					
Creating, merging, rearranging, deleting, and modifying layers					
Creating a guide layer					
Using the Timeline and frames in an animation					

Skill	1	2	3	4	5
Creating a frame-by-frame animation					
Using Onion Skin					
Creating a shape tweened animation					
Using shape hints					
Creating graphic symbols and editing symbols					
Using the Library panel					
Creating a motion tweened animation					
Controlling the speed of a motion tween					
Arranging and extending frames					
Creating, swapping, and duplicating button symbols					
Modifying button states					

Topic C: Re-keying the course

If you have the proper hardware and software, you can re-key this course after class. This section explains what you'll need in order to do so, and how to do it.

Computer requirements

To re-key this course, your personal computer must have:

- A keyboard and a mouse
- A Pentium III processor with minimum 600 MHz
- A minimum of 256 of MB RAM (512 MB recommended)
- A minimum of 800 MB of hard disk space
- A CD-ROM drive
- An XGA monitor or better, set at a minimum 1024x768 resolution
- 32-bit color display
- Internet access if you want to download data files from www.courseilt.com/instructor_tools.html

Setup instructions to re-key the course

Before you re-key the course, you will need to perform the following steps.

1 Install Microsoft Windows XP on an NTFS partition according to the software manufacturer's instructions. If you have Internet access, install the latest critical updates and service packs from www.windowsupdate.com. (You can also use Windows 2000, but the screen shots in this course were taken using Windows XP, so your screens might look somewhat different.)

2 Install Macromedia Flash MX 2004 according to the software manufacturer's instructions.

3 Activate Flash MX 2004 (product registration is not required).

   a Start Flash.

   b Enter the serial number, click Continue, and follow the remaining prompts.

   c Close Flash.

4 Adjust your computer's display properties as follows:

   a Right-click the desktop and choose Properties to open the Display Properties dialog box.

   b On the Settings tab, change the Color quality to 16 bit or higher, and the Screen resolution to 1024 by 768 pixels.

   c On the Appearance tab, set Windows and buttons to Windows XP style.

   d Click OK. If you are prompted to accept the new settings, click OK and click Yes. Then, if necessary, close the Display Properties dialog box.

5 Display file extensions.

   a Start Windows Explorer.

   b Choose Tools, Folder Options, and activate the View tab.

   c Clear Hide file extensions for known file types, and click OK.

   d Close Windows Explorer.

6 Create a folder called Student Data at the root of the hard drive (C:\).

7 Download the Student Data files for the course. You can download the data directly to your machine, to a central location on your own network, or to a disk.

    a   Connect to www.courseilt.com/instructor_tools.html.

    b   Click the link for Macromedia Flash to display a page of course listings, and then click the link for Flash MX 2004: Basic.

    c   Click the link for downloading the Student Data files, and follow the instructions that appear on your screen.

8 Copy the data files for the course to the Student Data folder.

Unit 1

Flash basics

Unit time: 60 minutes

Complete this unit, and you'll know how to:

A Start Flash, identify components of the Flash MX environment, and create a new Flash file.

B Identify the difference between raster and vector graphics, import and manipulate images, and convert a bitmap image to a vector image.

C Create lines and shapes by using the Pencil, Pen, and Line tools.

Topic A: The Flash interface

Explanation

Macromedia Flash MX 2004 enables you to integrate text, images, video, and audio into your Web projects and create animations and application interfaces. The power and flexibility of Flash have made it the most popular and pervasive software platform on the Web.

Components of the Flash application window

The following table describes the major components of the Flash environment:

Component	Description
Toolbox	Contains several tools for drawing, selecting, editing, coloring, and viewing images
Menu bar	Contains menus that you use to interact with Flash
Title bar	Displays the name of the application and the current document
Panels	Help you monitor, arrange, and modify Flash content; you view or hide the panels by using the Window menu

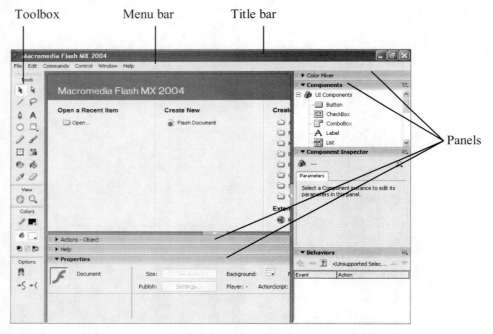

Exhibit 1-1: The Flash environment

The Toolbox

The Toolbox is divided into four sections:

- **Tools**: Contains tools for selecting, drawing, and editing shapes or images
- **View**: Contains tools that allow you to view an image in different modes
- **Colors**: Contains tools that allow you to apply and manage colors
- **Options**: Contains modifiers for each tool; the modifiers appear only when a tool is selected in the Tools section

The following table describes the functions of some of the more commonly used tools in the Toolbox:

Tool	Button	Description
Rectangle		Creates rectangles and squares
Text		Inserts a text block
Pencil		Draws freeform lines and shapes
Paint Bucket		Changes the fill color of shapes; *fill* defines the color inside an object
Eraser		Erases unwanted parts of a shape
Zoom		Magnifies a particular area of a drawing
Free Transform		Transforms images, instances, or text blocks; you can resize, rotate, distort, or envelop images, instances, or text blocks
Selection		Selects or moves an object

Panels

You use panels to modify the characteristics of Flash files, such as changing the height and width of images, selecting colors, or changing text settings. Panels include the Color Mixer, Components, Component Inspector, Behaviors, Actions- Object, Help, and Properties.

If you need more working space in the Flash application window, you can hide a panel. To hide a panel, double-click the title bar and the panel will minimize or maximize. To close a panel, right-click the panel, and choose Close Panel.

As you become acquainted with Flash, you might find that you use some panels more frequently than others. You can easily customize the panel layout and display only those panels that you want to use regularly. You can then save your customized panel layout by choosing Window, Save Panel Layout. You open your panel set by choosing Window, Panel Set, and then the name of your panel set.

The following table describes some of the most commonly used panels.

Panel	Name	Description
	Color Mixer	Use this panel to create and edit solid colors and gradient fills, create new colors, and adjust the alpha of existing colors. A color's *alpha* is its degree of transparency.
	Properties	Also known as the *Property inspector*. The options in the Property inspector change according to the object that's selected. You use it to customize font properties, move objects, add sound, view information about a selection, and apply a variety of other properties.
	Components	Contains user interface components that you can drag into a Flash file. It includes several standard components, such as Button, CheckBox, and ProgressBar.
	Help	Use this panel to view a comprehensive array of topics related to working in Flash. It contains two tabs, Help and How Do I. The Help tab contains the Contents, Index, and Search buttons. The How Do I tab contains Help lessons and tutorials, which are organized into three folders: Quick Start, Basic Flash, and Basic ActionScript.

Do it!

A-1: Exploring the Flash interface

Here's how	Here's why
1 Choose **Start**, **All Programs**, **Macromedia**, **Macromedia Flash MX 2004**	To start Flash MX 2004. You'll explore the Flash interface.
2 Locate the Menu bar	It contains standard options like File, Edit, and View, and Flash-specific menu options like Commands and Control.
3 Locate the Toolbox	Tools like Lasso, Pen, Rectangle, Free Transform, and Zoom allow you to take a particular action on a Flash file.
4 Locate the panels	By default, Flash displays seven panels: Color Mixer, Components, Component Inspector, Behaviors, Actions- Object, Help, and Properties.

Creating new Flash files

Explanation

To create a new Flash file:

1 Choose File, New to open the New Document dialog box, as shown in Exhibit 1-2.
2 On the General tab, select Flash Document.
3 Click OK.

A Flash file with a .fla extension is created.

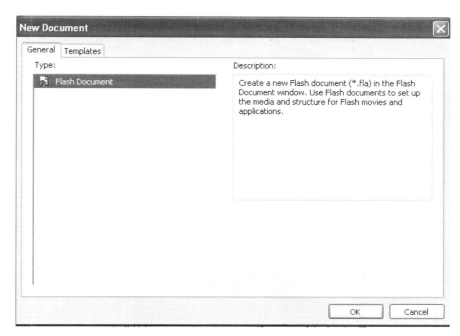

Exhibit 1-2: The New Document dialog box

Flash files and the Flash workspace

When you create or open a Flash file, other features of the application workspace appear, including the Stage, the Timeline window, and the Zoom box. The following table provides a brief overview of some of these workspace components, which are shown in Exhibit 1-3.

Component	Description
Timeline	Controls a document's content and organizes it into a sequence of frames, layers, and the *playhead*, which indicates the current frame on the Stage.
Stage	Is the rectangular area where you create and modify a Flash document.
Zoom box	Displays the current magnification of the image relative to its actual size. You can change the magnification by either selecting a magnification value from the Zoom list, or by entering a value directly in the Zoom box. By default, documents are displayed at 100%, or actual size.
Scrollbars	Allow you to view a document that doesn't fit into the available space on the Stage. You use the vertical scrollbar to scroll up or down on the Stage and the horizontal scrollbar to scroll left or right.

Toolbox   Menu bar   Timeline   Zoom box

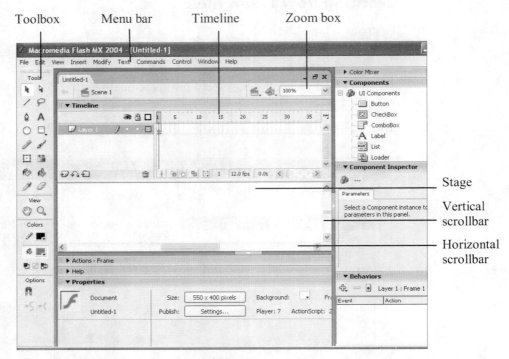

Exhibit 1-3: The Flash environment displaying an empty Flash file

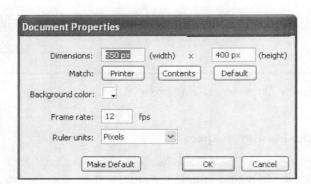

Exhibit 1-4: The Document Properties dialog box

Do it!

A-2: Creating a new Flash file

Here's how	Here's why
1 Choose **File, New...**	To open the New Document dialog box.
2 Click **OK**	To create a new Flash file.
3 Locate the Stage	(Refer to Exhibit 1-3.) You'll spend most of your development time in the Stage.
4 Choose **File, Save As...**	To open the Save As dialog box.

5 From the Save in list, select the
   current unit folder

6 In the File name box, enter
   MyFlashDocument

   Observe the Save as type list

   By default, Flash MX 2004 Document (*.fla) is
   selected.

   Click **Save**

   To save the file.

7 Choose **Modify, Document...**

   To open the Document Properties dialog box, as
   shown in Exhibit 1-4. By default, documents
   have a width of 550 pixels and a height of 400
   pixels. You will customize the dimensions of
   this document.

8 In the Dimensions box for width,
   enter **800 px**

   To specify a new document width.

   In the Dimensions box for height,
   enter **600 px**

   To specify a new document height.

9 Click the Background color down-
   arrow as indicated

   Select any color

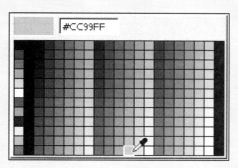

   Click **OK**

   The document's dimensions and background
   color change accordingly. The background color
   you specify will be the background color of the
   entire Flash document.

10 Choose **File, Save**

   To save your changes.

Topic B: Working with images

Explanation

You can import images from other applications such as Fireworks, Freehand, and Photoshop, and use several different image file formats, including EPS, GIF, JPG, and BMP. These are file types for raster images. In Flash, you create vector images. Therefore, to modify an imported raster image, you must first convert it to a vector image.

Raster and vector graphics

There are two general images types, raster and vector. *Raster graphics*, such as bitmaps, GIF, and JPG files, are based on a grid of pixels. A *pixel* is the smallest measurable unit in a screen image. Raster graphics are resolution-dependent, which means that when you enlarge a raster image, the size of the pixel increases, giving the picture a jagged look. Graphics software such as Adobe Photoshop, Macromedia Fireworks, and Corel Photo Paint are popular tools for creating raster images.

Vector graphics are based on mathematically defined points, lines, and curves called vectors. Vector graphics are resolution-independent, which means that when you resize, rotate, magnify, or transform them, they retain their original clarity. Vector graphics require less storage space than raster graphics, and they are scalable and portable. Flash makes it easy to create and edit vector graphics.

Do it!

B-1: Discussing bitmap and vector graphics

Questions and answers
1 What is the difference between raster and vector graphics?
2 What is a pixel?
3 What does resolution-independent signify?
4 What does resolution-dependent signify?

Importing images

Explanation

To import an image file:

1   Choose File, Import, Import to Stage to open the Import dialog box.
2   In the Files of type list, verify that All Formats is selected.
3   Select the image you want to import, and click Open.

The Free Transform tool

You use the Free Transform tool to rotate, skew, scale, or distort lines and shapes. When you select an object by using the Free Transform tool, a square box appears at each corner and on all sides of the image, as shown in Exhibit 1-5. These square boxes are called *handles*. The handle on each corner is called a *corner handle*, and the handle on each side is called an *edge handle*.

Exhibit 1-5: Handles on an image

A small circle also appears at the center of the image. This is called the *transformation point*. When you set a transformation point, any action you take will take place around that point—it will not move on the Stage. This helps you to precisely scale, skew, and rotate an image. When you select the Free Transform tool, its modifiers appear in the Options section of the Toolbox. The following table describes the modifiers of the Free Transform tool.

Modifier	Button	Description
Rotate and Skew		Rotates or slants an image along one or both axes
Scale		Resizes an image
Distort		Changes the size and shape of an object
Envelope		Warps shape objects; an envelope contains one or more objects and if its shape is changed, the shapes of all objects inside it change

To transform objects freely:

1   Click the Free Transform tool.
2   Drag the pointer over the object to form a bounding box.
3   Click the modifier you want to apply to the object.

B-2: Importing and manipulating images

Here's how	Here's why
1 Right-click the title bar of the Components panel	
Choose **Close Panel**	To increase the working area of the Stage.
2 Close the other side panels	Right-click the title bars of each panel and choose Close Panel.
3 Click the indicated down-arrow on the bottom panel	
	To hide the panels at the bottom of the Flash window.
4 Choose **File**, **Import**, **Import to Stage...**	To open the Import dialog box.
5 Verify that the current unit folder is selected	
Verify that All Formats is selected	In the Files of type list.
6 Select **tableSetting.png**	This is a PNG file, which is a raster image.
Click **Open**	The image appears on the Stage.
7 Click the image once	
	To select it. A gray box delineates the boundaries of the selection.
From the Zoom list, select **400%**	
	The enlarged image appears blurry and jagged because raster images lose quality when they are resized.
Change the Zoom setting to **100%**	To return the image to its original size.

8 Drag the image toward the center
   of the Stage

9 Click

(In the Toolbox.) To activate the Free Transform
tool. The handles and transformation point
appear.

Observe the Options section

Two modifiers are available, Rotate and Skew
and Scale. The Distort and Envelope modifiers
cannot be used on bitmap images.

Click

To select the Scale modifier. You'll resize the
image.

10 Point to the lower-right corner
    handle as shown

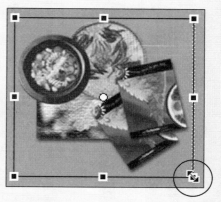

Dragging the corner handles will change the
height and width of the object proportionately.

Drag the corner handle slightly
downward and to the right, and
release

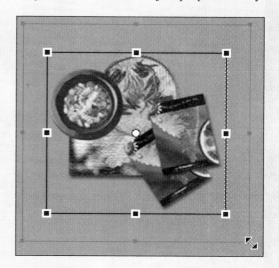

To increase the size of the image. The image
appears slightly blurry.

11 Point to the right edge handle

Dragging the edge handle to the left or right changes the width of the object. Dragging the edge handle inward or outward from top or bottom changes the height of the object.

Drag the right edge handle slightly to the right

To increase the width of the image.

12 Point to the transformation point

(In the center of the image.) The position of the transformation point can be changed for scaling, skewing, or rotating graphic objects precisely.

Drag the transformation point down and to the right as shown

To change its position.

13 Click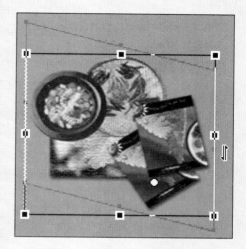

(In the Toolbox.) To select the Rotate and Skew modifier.

Drag the right edge handle slightly downward and release

To skew the image. Note that the transformation point does not move; the image skews around it, like a pressure point keeping it in place.

Double-click the transformation point

To restore it to the object's center.

14 Drag the left edge handle slightly downward and release

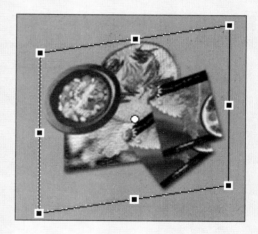

15 Deselect the image

Click anywhere on the Stage.

Save your changes

Tracing bitmaps

Explanation

The Trace Bitmap command allows you to convert a bitmap image (a BMP, JPG, GIF, or PNG file) into a vector graphic. When you convert a bitmap (raster) image to a vector graphic, Flash creates many shapes that reproduce, in variable accuracy, the original image. In Flash, you can do much more with a vector graphic than you can with a bitmap image. After you have converted a bitmap image to a vector image, you can manipulate it in a variety of ways. Converting a bitmap to a vector image will often decrease the image's file size as well. However, to reproduce some images, a large number of shapes must be created, which can actually increase the file size in comparison.

To trace a bitmap image:

1 Select the imported image.

2 Choose Modify, Bitmap, Trace Bitmap to open the Trace Bitmap dialog box, as shown in Exhibit 1-6.

3 Specify your desired settings and click OK.

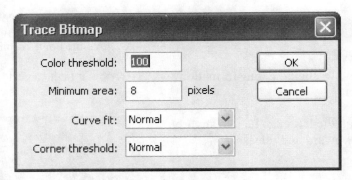

Exhibit 1-6: The Trace Bitmap dialog box

The following table describes the options in the Trace Bitmap dialog box.

Option	Description
Color threshold	Determines the accuracy with which colors are converted to a vector image. Values range from 1 to 500. The closer the value is to 500, the fewer the number of transferred colors, meaning the image will look less like the original. A value of 1 creates the closest available match to the original bitmap image.
Minimum area	Determines the size of each shape generated by Flash in the conversion from a bitmap to a vector graphic. This value can vary from 1 to 1000. The smaller the number, the smaller the shapes, which results in more image detail.
Curve fit	Has six predefined values that determine the degree with which the individual vector shapes match the original bitmap image colors. The Very Smooth value creates longer curves, and typically produces a closer quality match to the original image.
Corner threshold	Has three predefined values that determine the degree to which a curve can bend before it becomes two separate curves. The Many Corners value produces smoother lines, and typically produces a closer quality match to the original image.

Depending on the settings you choose, the bitmap image you're converting, and your computer's processing power, it might take a while to convert a bitmap to a vector graphic. For example, if you set the Color threshold value to 1, the Minimum area value to 1, the Curve fit value to Very Smooth, and the Corner threshold value to Many Corners, Flash will create the closest possible match to the original image, which can require a large amount of processing and result in a large file size. You need to determine the right balance between image clarity and file size.

Zooming in on shapes

When you use the Zoom tool or the Zoom box, only the shape's display changes, not its actual dimensions or file size. From the Zoom box, you can select magnification levels ranging from 25% to 800%, or you can specify your own magnification level by entering a value directly in the Zoom box. When you select the Zoom tool, the Enlarge and Reduce modifiers appear in the Options section of the Toolbox. By default, the Enlarge modifier is selected. If you select the Enlarge modifier, pressing the Alt key toggles the Zoom to Reduce, and vice versa.

Do it!

B-3: Converting bitmaps to vector graphics

Here's how	Here's why
1 Select the image	Click it once.
Choose **Modify**, **Bitmap**, **Trace Bitmap...**	To open the Trace Bitmap dialog box. You'll convert the image to a vector graphic.
In the Color threshold box, enter **60**	To set the accuracy with which colors are converted. The lower the number from 1 to 500, the higher the degree of resulting image quality.
In the Minimum area box, enter **100**	To set the size of each shape generated by Flash as it converts the bitmap to a vector graphic. The lower the number from 1 to 1000, the higher the degree of resulting image quality.
2 From the Curve fit list, select **Smooth**	To set the degree with which the individual vector shapes will match the original bitmap image colors.
From the Corner threshold list, select **Many corners**	To use smooth lines and create a higher quality image than the default value for this option.
Click **OK**	To convert the image. Flash briefly displays a progress bar as it converts the image to a vector graphic.
Deselect the image	(Click an empty area on the Stage.) The image is converted into a vector image. It no longer consists of pixels, but mathematical shapes, lines, and curves. The quality of this image will not change if its size increases or decreases.

3 Click 🔍	(The Zoom tool is on the Toolbox, under View.) You will magnify the image.
Click the image twice	The image is magnified. Note that there is no change in the image quality like there is when you magnify a bitmap (raster) image.
4 Press and hold (ALT)	You will zoom out without switching tools first.
Click the image twice	To zoom out and return to the original view at 100%.
Release (ALT)	
5 Save your changes	
6 Close the file	Choose File, Close.

Topic C: Basic drawing

Explanation

You use the Pencil and Pen tools to create vector art, such as curves, lines, and custom shapes. Flash makes it easier to create manual drawings than you might think. By using the right line settings, you can draw smooth curves, perfectly straight lines, and other things that might seem difficult to achieve manually.

The Pencil tool

You use the Pencil tool to draw lines and create shapes. There are three drawing modes available for the Pencil tool: Straighten, Smooth, and Ink. These modes are used to draw straight, smooth curved, and freehand lines respectively.

To use the Pencil tool to create shapes:

1   From the Toolbox, select the Pencil tool. The pointer appears as a pencil when placed anywhere over the Stage. The Pencil mode button also appears in the Options section of the Toolbox.

2   Click the Pencil mode button, and select a mode from the list.

3   Point to where you want to start drawing.

4   Drag the pencil to start a line or shape.

Line drawing options

When you activate the Pencil tool, the Pencil mode button appears in the Options section of the Toolbox. Exhibit 1-7 demonstrates the results of three modes you can use. When you select the Straighten mode, any line you draw will be straight. When you select Smooth, any flaws in the line you draw will be smoothed over. When you select Ink mode, your line will not be modified in any way—what you create is precisely what you get.

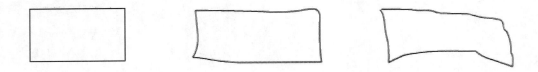

Exhibit 1-7: A drawing in Straighten, Smooth, and Ink mode

The Eraser tool

You use the Eraser tool to remove parts of a line or shape. The Eraser tool erases specific individual stroke segments, specific filled areas on the Stage, or everything on the Stage. To erase everything on the Stage, double-click the Eraser tool.

When you select the Eraser tool, its modifiers appear in the Options section of the Toolbox. There are three modifiers for the Eraser tool:

- **The Faucet modifier**: Allows you to erase strokes or fill areas. A *stroke* is the line or curve of a shape. For example, you use the Faucet modifier when you want to erase the fill of a rectangle but not the stroke. To use the Faucet modifier, select the Eraser tool, then select the Faucet modifier and click the portion of the line or shape that you want to erase.

- **The Eraser Shape modifier**: Allows you to select a desired eraser size and shape, which can help you erase more precisely by using a small eraser, or erase with fast, broad strokes by using a large eraser.

- **The Eraser Mode modifier**: Allows you to erase a particular part of a line or shape depending on the option you select from the drop-down list.

The following table describes the available Eraser modes:

Mode	Description
Erase Normal	Erases strokes and fills when you drag the Eraser tool over them
Erase Fills	Erases only fills; lines are not affected
Erase Lines	Erases only lines; fills are not affected
Erase Selected Fills	Erases only the fills that you have selected; all other fills are not affected, nor are any lines
Erase Inside	Erases an entire fill area, and does not affect any fills outside the selected shape

C-1:   Applying the Pencil and Eraser tools

Here's how	Here's why
1 Create a new Flash document	Choose File, New, and click OK.
2 Choose **Modify**, **Document...**	To open the Document Properties dialog box.
Select a background color	
Click **OK**	
3 Save the document as **MyPencil**	(In the current unit folder.) Choose File, Save As. Enter MyPencil in the file name box, and click Save.
4 Click	(In the Toolbox.) To activate the Pencil tool.
5 Under Options, click	To display a drop-down list with the three options: Straighten, Smooth, and Ink.
6 From the Pencil Mode list, select **Smooth**	To smooth the lines you draw.
7 Point to an empty space on the Stage and draw as shown	
	Note that Flash automatically makes the line smooth when you finish dragging it.
8 Draw two more lines as shown	
9 Draw lines to create a leaf as shown	

10 Click   (In the Toolbox.) To activate the Eraser tool.

11 Under Options, display the Eraser
    Shape list

You can choose from several different Eraser shapes. Select a small brush if you want to erase small areas, or a large brush to erase larger areas of an image.

12 From the list, select the smallest
    square as shown

The eraser will use this shape and size to erase your lines, shapes, and colors.

    Point anywhere on the Stage

The pointer changes to the selected shape.

13 Drag over a line on the drawing

The erased area appears white.

14 Choose a different Eraser shape

    Erase another portion of the image

15 Save and close the file

The Pen tool

Explanation

By using the Pen tool, you can create an open or closed path. An *open path* is a straight or curved line whose start and end points do not meet. A *closed path* is a line whose start and end points meet to create a closed loop. For example, a rectangle, an ellipse, a square, and a polygon are all closed paths, while a straight line or a spiral are examples of an open path.

When you draw with the Pen tool, you click to create distinct points that create lines. These points and the line or shape they create is called a path. You can also click and drag to create curves, and adjust your lines and curves with a precision that's difficult to achieve by using a freehand tool. A path consists of segments and anchor points. Exhibit 1-8 shows a path and its various components.

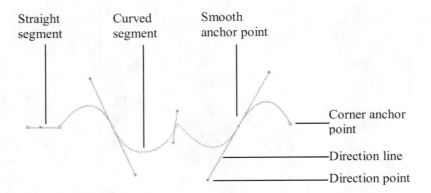

Exhibit 1-8: A path and its components

The following table describes the various components of a path when you use the Pen tool:

Component	Description
Segment	The smallest building block of a path. It can be a straight line or a curved line.
Anchor point	Defines the end points of a segment. It's a small, square point that links two segments to create a path. It contributes to the sharpness, smoothness, and direction of curves and lines. There are two types of anchor points, smooth and corner, which differ based on their direction lines and direction points.
Direction line	Defines the height or depth and the direction of a curve. The longer the direction line, the greater the height or depth in that direction.
Direction point	Defines the end of a direction line. It's a small circle that you drag to increase, decrease, or move the line. The more you drag it away from an anchor point, the longer the direction line will be.
Smooth anchor point	Links two curved segments such that the second curve appears to be a continuation of the first. Both direction lines at this anchor point are constrained by each other at 180 degrees. If you increase, decrease, or move one direction line, the other changes proportionately in the opposite direction, maintaining the smoothness of the curve.
Corner anchor point	Joins two curved or straight segments or a straight and a curved segment in such a way that a point appears at the joint on the path. It can have one, two, or zero direction lines. The direction lines are not constrained by each other, and you can modify a segment of a path without affecting the other parts of the path.

To create a path by using the Pen tool:

1 Activate the Pen tool. The pointer changes to a pen.

2 Click where you want to start the path. An anchor point appears.

3 Drag the mouse in the desired direction. As you drag, the direction lines for the anchor point appear. The longer the direction line, the greater the segment's curve. To create a straight segment, click and release the mouse button.

4 Click where you want to place the end point of the segment and drag the direction line. A curved segment appears that connects the first anchor point with the current one. You can adjust the curve of the segment by dragging one of the direction lines.

5 To create a closed path, click the first anchor point and drag to adjust the curve. A curved segment appears that connects the last anchor point with the first.

Do it!

C-2:   Drawing with the Pen tool

Here's how	Here's why
1 Create a new Flash file	
Save the file as **PenTool**	In the current unit folder.
2 Give the document a background color of your choice	Choose Modify, Document, click the Background color box, select a color, and click OK.
3 Click [pen icon]	(In the Toolbox.) To activate the Pen tool.
4 Click an empty area on the left of the Stage	To create the starting anchor point. An anchor point links two segments to create a path.
5 Point to an area above and to the right of the anchor point	

6 Drag toward the lower-right corner of the Stage as shown

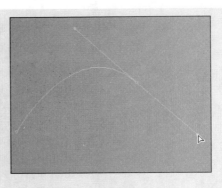

As you drag the pointer, two line segments appear on opposite sides of a small circle. These are the direction lines.

7 Release the mouse button

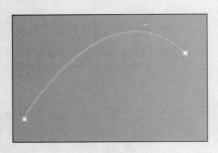

Flash draws a curve based on the points and the direction line. You will continue with this drawing to create a leaf.

8 Point to the original anchor point as shown

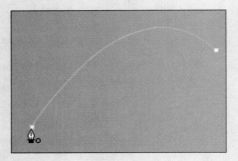

9 Drag to the upper left as shown

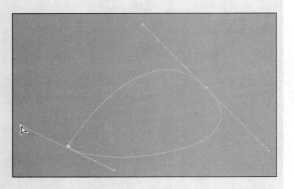

As you drag the direction line, the line segment connecting the two anchor points forms a new curve.

10 Release the mouse button

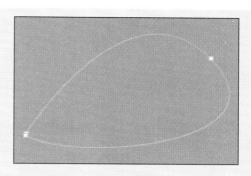

The leaf begins to take shape.

11 Click inside the leaf to create another point as shown

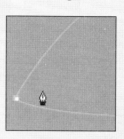

12 Point to the upper-right area of the shape as shown

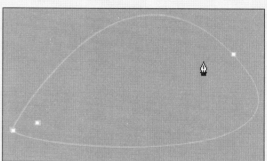

13 Click and drag towards the lower-right corner as shown

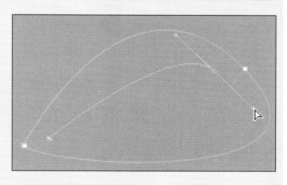

14 Release the mouse button

The general shape of a leaf appears.

15 Save and close the document

The Line tool

You use the Line tool to draw straight lines. To draw a line:

1 From the Toolbox, select the Line tool.
2 Point to the area on the Stage where you want to start the line. The pointer changes to a plus sign.
3 Drag to draw the line and release the mouse button to complete the line.

Viewing rulers

Rulers can help you to precisely create and position shapes on the Stage. Rulers appear along the top and left side of the work area. To view them, choose View, Rulers.

Rulers track the pointer's position on the Stage. By default, divisions on the rulers are in pixels. You can change the measurement units to millimeters, centimeters, points, or inches. To set the ruler units, choose Modify, Document to open the Document Properties dialog box. Select a unit from the Ruler Units list, and click OK.

Do it!

C-3: Creating custom line styles

Here's how	Here's why
1 Create a new Flash document	
Save the file as **MyRuler**	
2 Choose **View**, **Rulers**	To show the rulers. They appear along the top and left side of the Stage.
3 Choose **Modify**, **Document...**	To open the Document Properties dialog box.
From the Ruler units list, select **Inches**	To change the scale of the ruler to inches.
4 Click **OK**	
Observe the ruler	It is now divided by inches.
5 Click [✐]	(In the Toolbox.) To activate the Line tool. You'll draw straight-line segments.
6 Point to the Stage at the one inch by one inch mark, as shown	You will draw a horizontal line.

7   Drag to the right about an inch and a half

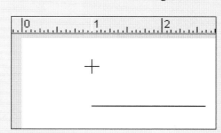

To draw a horizontal line segment.

8   Point as shown

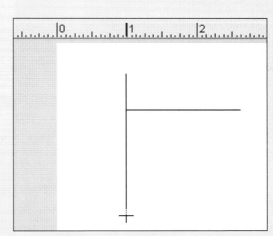

(To the 1-inch mark on the top ruler and the 0.5-inch mark on the left ruler.) You will draw a vertical line.

9   Drag downward

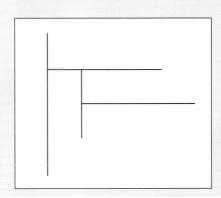

To draw a vertical line. Release the mouse when the line reaches the 2.5-inch mark on the left ruler.

10   Draw two more lines as shown

11	Choose **Window**, **Properties**	To view the Properties panel, which is more commonly referred to as the Property inspector.
	Expand the Properties panel	If necessary.
12	Click **Custom**	

(On the Property inspector.) To open the Stroke Style dialog box.

13	From the Thickness list, select **2**	To increase the thickness of the line.
	Check **Sharp corners**	

To make the corners sharp.

	From the Type list, select **Ragged**	Note that additional options appear. You will create a ragged line.
14	Click **OK**	
15	Point and drag as shown	

To draw a horizontal line with a ragged style.

	Release the mouse button and observe the line	

A bold, ragged line appears.

16	Save your changes and close the file	

Unit summary: Flash basics

Topic A   In this topic, you learned about the components of the Flash environment. You learned how to create and save a new Flash file and how to specify the **dimensions** and **background color** of a document.

Topic B   In this topic, you learned the difference between **raster** and **vector graphics**, and you learned how to import and manipulate images. You also learned how to use the **Free Transform tool** and its **modifiers**. Finally, you learned how to convert a bitmap (raster) image to a vector image.

Topic C   In this topic, you learned how to create lines and curves by using the Pencil and Pen tools. You also learned how to use the Eraser tool, and create straight lines by using the Line tool. Finally, you learned about using rulers to help create more precise lines or curves, and you learned how to apply basic **line styles**.

Independent practice activity

1 Create a new Flash document.

2 Save the file as **MyPractice.**

3 Draw the chili pepper shown in Exhibit 1-9 by using the Pencil tool.

4 Save your changes, share your results, and close the document. Don't close Flash.

Exhibit 1-9: A simple chili drawing

Unit 2
Shapes

Unit time: 80 minutes

Complete this unit, and you'll know how to:

A Create a variety of shapes, create rounded edges, use the rulers to create precise shape sizes, and create freeform shapes.

B Use the Selection, Subselection, and Lasso tools, change line styles, transform shapes, copy, move, and delete a shape, and group shapes.

Topic A: Basic shapes

Explanation

You can create basic shapes such as rectangles, ovals, and circles by using the shape tools. To create squares and rectangles, you use the Rectangle tool. To create ovals and circles, you use the Oval tool.

Drawing basic shapes

To create a rectangle:

1   Select the Rectangle tool.
2   Point to where you want to start drawing the rectangle.
3   Drag diagonally until the rectangle is the desired size.

To draw a square, press and hold the Shift key before or while you drag. This will ensure that you draw a perfect square.

You can also draw rectangles and squares with rounded corners by using the Round Rectangle Radius modifier. To use this modifier:

1   Select the Rectangle tool. The Round Rectangle Radius modifier appears in the Options section of the Toolbox.
2   Click the Round Rectangle Radius modifier to open the Rectangle Settings dialog box. In the dialog box, specify the desired Corner Radius and click OK.
3   Point to where you want to start drawing the rectangle.
4   Drag diagonally until the rectangle is the desired size.

To draw ovals and circles:

1   Select the Oval tool.
2   Point to where you want to start drawing the oval.
3   Drag diagonally until the oval is the desired size.

To draw a circle, press and hold the Shift key before or while you drag. This will ensure that you draw a perfect circle.

Fill colors

When you draw a shape, the currently selected fill color will fill the inside of the shape. To customize the fill color of a shape you are about to draw, click the Fill Color box, shown in Exhibit 2-1, and select the desired color from the palette that pops up.

Exhibit 2-1: The Fill Color box

Do it!

A-1: Creating rectangles, ovals, and circles

Here's how	Here's why
1 Create a new Flash document	Choose File, New to open the New dialog box, and click OK.
2 Save the document as **Shapes**	In the current unit folder.
3 Verify that the Property inspector is displayed	
Select the Line tool	(If necessary.) You'll adjust the stroke style.
4 Click Custom	(On the Property inspector.) To open the Stroke Style dialog box.
From the Thickness list, select **1**	(If necessary.) To decrease the thickness of the line.
Clear Sharp corners	
5 From the Type list, select **Solid**	
Click **OK**	To apply the Line settings.
6 Hide any active panels	
7 From the Zoom box, select **Show Frame**	
	To display the entire Stage on the screen.
8 Display the rulers	Choose View, Rulers.
9 Click	(In the Toolbox.) To activate the Rectangle tool.

10 Click the Fill Color box

(In the Colors section of the Tools panel.) A color palette appears.

   Select a light fill color

This will be the fill color for the rectangle you draw.

11 Change the scale of the ruler to inches

Choose Modify, Document. From the Ruler units list, select Inches, and click OK.

12 Point to 1,1 on the Stage, as shown

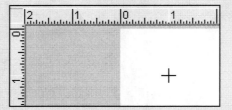

You'll draw a rectangle starting at this point.

   Drag toward the lower-right corner of the Stage to point 7,5

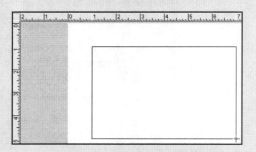

Release the mouse button when the upper ruler indicates a width of 7 inches, and the left ruler indicates a height of 5 inches.

   Observe the rectangle

It appears with your chosen fill color.

13 Starting at 1.5 on both axes, draw another rectangle to 6.5, 4.5 as shown

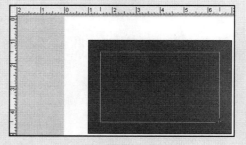

To draw a rectangle inside the first rectangle.

14 Under Options, click

(The Round Rectangle Radius modifier is under the Options section in the Toolbox.) To open the Rectangle Settings dialog box. You specify the corner radius for a round rectangle in this dialog box. By default, the box reads 0.

   Enter **12**

To specify the corner radius as 12 points. You'll draw a rectangle with rounded corners.

   Click **OK**

To close the dialog box.

15 Draw another rectangle inside the second rectangle

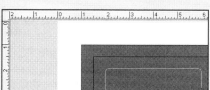

The rectangle appears with rounded corners.

16 Click

(In the Toolbox.) To activate the Oval tool.

17 Point to 2,4 and drag to point 6,4.5 as shown

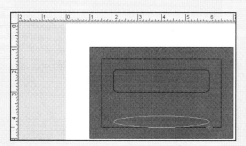

To draw an oval on the Stage.

   Press (SHIFT)

You'll draw a circle.

   Point to inside the rectangle and drag

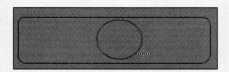

A circle appears inside the rectangle.

18 Save your changes and close the document

Freeform shapes

Explanation

You can create freeform shapes by using the Pencil and Pen tools. Use the Property inspector to customize the style, height, and color of the lines you draw.

Do it!

A-2: Creating freeform shapes

Here's how	Here's why
1 Create a new Flash document	
Save the document as **Pepper**	In the current unit folder.
2 Activate the Pencil tool	
Change the document size to **100%**	If necessary.
Under Options, from the list, select	(The Ink option.) This Pencil style helps you draw freeform shapes that do not straighten or smooth out.
3 Point to an empty spot on the Stage	You'll create a freeform shape.
4 Drag to draw a shape as shown	
5 Extend the shape as shown	
6 Complete the shape to create the outline of a chili pepper as shown	

7 Draw wavy lines inside the chili, as shown

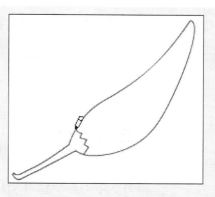

To draw the stem of the chili.

8 Save and close the document

Topic B: Selecting and editing shapes

Explanation

Before you can move or modify a shape, you need to select it. Flash provides three tools that enable you to select a shape: the Selection, Subselection, and Lasso tools. When a shape is selected, its fill area appears dotted to indicate that it's selected. After you select a shape, you can transform it by using the Selection and Free Transform tools. If you want to change the magnification of a shape while you transform it, use the Zoom and Hand tools. You can also reposition, copy, move, or delete shapes.

The Selection tool

The Selection tool enables you to select a shape in a variety of ways. For example, you can select only the fill area of a shape, only its stroke, or both. To use the Selection tool to select:

- **Only a shape's stroke**: Point to an area of the stroke. The pointer will show a curve or corner line, as shown in Exhibit 2-2. When the curve or corner line appears, click once to select only that segment of the stroke, or double-click to select the entire stroke of the shape.

- **Only the fill**: Click anywhere inside the shape. The shape's fill area will appear dotted to indicate that it's selected.

- **The entire shape**: Double-click anywhere inside the shape.

- **Multiple shapes or strokes of multiple shapes**: Press and hold the Shift key and select each shape or stroke individually.

Exhibit 2-2: The corner line under the pointer helps you select a stroke

The Subselection tool

You use the Subselection tool to display the anchor points of any drawn shape. You can then use these anchor points to change the appearance of the shape. To use the Subselection tool, select the tool and click a shape to display its anchor points, as demonstrated in Exhibit 2-3.

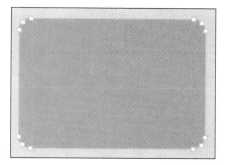

Exhibit 2-3: Anchor points on a rounded rectangle

Marquee selections

You also use the Selection tool or the Subselection tool to select a rectangular marquee. A *Marquee selection* helps you select multiple shapes or only those parts of a shape that you want to modify.

To select a rectangular marquee:

1 Activate the Selection or Subselection tool.
2 Point to where you want to start the selection.
3 Drag to select the desired shapes. As you drag, a rectangle appears that indicates the selection area.
4 Release the mouse where you want the selection to stop. The rectangle disappears, and the shapes appear selected.

B-1: Using the Selection and Lasso tools

Here's how	Here's why
1 Open Chili.fla	From the current unit folder.
2 Save the file as **MyChili**	In the current unit folder.
3 From the Zoom list, select **Fit in Window**	To view the entire Stage.
4 Click ⬉	(In the Toolbox.) To activate the Selection tool.
5 Click the rounded rectangle as shown	(At the bottom of the Stage.) Only the top line of the shape is selected.
Press (ESC)	To deselect the line.
6 Point to the left edge of the rounded rectangle	A curved line appears underneath the pointer, indicating that it will select only a segment within the rounded rectangle.
Click once	Only that segment of the stroke is selected.
Double-click the same spot	The entire stroke is selected.
Press (ESC)	To deselect the shape.

7	Click ▲	(In the Toolbox.) To activate the Subselection tool.
	Click any area of the oval stroke	
		The anchor points appear and the selection turns green, indicating a subselection has been made.
	Deselect the shape	Press Esc.
8	Click ◯	(In the Toolbox.) To activate the Lasso tool. The pointer changes to a lasso.
9	Drag the lasso around two shapes	
		As you drag the pointer, a line is drawn.
	Release the mouse button	
		The shapes inside the line are selected.
10	Open the Property inspector	
11	Display the Stroke style list	
	Select the indicated line style	

12 Deselect the shapes

(Click anywhere on the Stage.) Instead of a solid line, the strokes appear "sketchy."

13 Save your changes

Minimize the document

Transform shapes

Explanation

You transform shapes by using the Selection and Free Transform tools. For example, you can create the shape of a mango from an oval by pulling one of its sides inward, or you can create the shape of a diamond by editing the corners of a rectangle by using the Free Transform tool.

To edit the curves and corners of a shape, select the Free Transform tool and point to the line segment that you want to reshape. A corner or curve appears underneath the pointer, indicating that it will select a straight or curved segment. You click to select that segment, or drag to modify the shape.

The Hand tool

After you have zoomed in on a shape, it's likely that you will only be able to view a small part of the total shape. However, you can use the Hand tool to move the Stage to view the other regions of the shape. To move the Stage, select the Hand tool and drag the Stage in the direction you want to move it.

Do it!

B-2:   Transforming shapes

Here's how	Here's why
1 Open Edit shapes.fla	From the current unit folder.
2 Save the file as **My Edit shapes**	In the current unit folder.
3 Maximize the document	If necessary.
Close the Property inspector	If necessary.
Change the zoom setting to **50%**	
4 Click [🔍]	To activate the Zoom tool.
Under Options, verify that [🔍] is selected	By default, the Enlarge tool is activated.
Click once inside the red oval	

To zoom in on the shape.

5 Activate the Selection tool	
6 Point as shown	

The pointer changes to an arrow with a curve at its tail end.

Drag downward

Release the mouse button

To modify the shape.

7 Point as shown

Drag slightly downward

Release the mouse button

8 Double-click the shape   To select the entire shape.

9 Activate the Free Transform tool

Under Options, click   To select the Rotate and Skew tool. You'll rotate the shape.

Point as shown

The pointer changes to a counter-clockwise arrow, indicating the direction of the rotation.

Drag as shown

10 In the Options section, click   You'll resize the shape.

     Point as shown

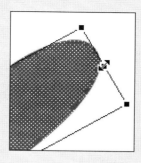

The pointer changes to a double-headed arrow.

     Drag toward the lower-left corner

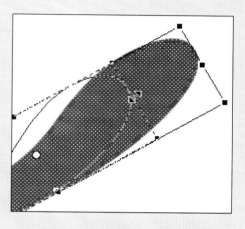

To resize the selected shape.

11 Press (ESC)   To deselect the shape, which now looks like a chili pepper.

12 Click [ ]   To select the Subselection tool. You'll make the anchor points of a shape visible and modify the shape.

     Click as shown

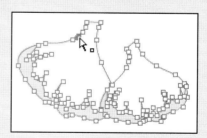

The anchor points and the direction lines for the shape are now visible.

13 Activate the Zoom tool

Point as shown

Drag as shown

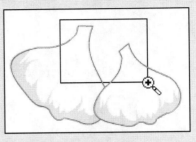

Release the mouse button   To zoom in on the selected region.

14 Activate the Subselection tool

Click as shown

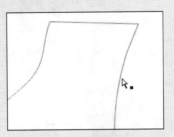

Direction lines appear on both sides of each
anchor point.

Point as shown

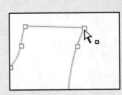

Drag as shown

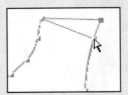

As you drag, the stroke of the shape moves
accordingly.

15 Click anywhere on the Stage	To deselect the shape, which is now updated.
16 Click [hand]	To activate the Hand tool.
Click anywhere on the Stage and drag to the upper-left edge of the Stage	To view the other areas of the drawing that are not visible due to the current magnification setting.
17 Change the magnification of the Stage to **Show Frame**	
Save and close the document	

Copying shapes

Explanation

If you want to duplicate a shape for use at another location in a document or in another document, you can create a copy of the shape as follows:

1 Select the shape.
2 Choose Edit, Copy. (Or Press Ctrl+C.)
3 Choose Edit, Paste. (Or Press Ctrl+V.) The copied shape appears in the center of the Stage.

Moving shapes

To move a shape is to change its position on the Stage. You can move a shape by using:

- **The Selection tool**: Select the tool, double-click the shape, and then drag it to the desired location on the Stage.
- **The keyboard arrow keys**: Select the shape and then press the arrow key that corresponds to the direction in which you want to move the shape.
- **The Property inspector**: Select the shape. The X and Y property boxes on the Property inspector become active. The X value refers to the selection's horizontal position on the Stage. The Y value refers to the selection's vertical position on the Stage. When you enter values, the selection moves to the new position. If you enter an invalid integer value in either the X or Y box, Flash prompts you to enter a valid value.

Deleting shapes

To delete a shape, select it by using the Selection tool and choose Edit, Clear, or press the Delete or Backspace key. You can delete multiple shapes by selecting all of them and then choosing Edit, Clear, or by pressing Delete or Backspace.

Do it!

B-3:   Copying, moving, and deleting a shape

Here's how	Here's why
1 Maximize the MyChili document	(If necessary.) You'll use this document to explore copying and moving shapes.
2 Activate the Selection tool	
3 Select the leaf shape	Drag to draw a rectangular selection around the leaf.
4 Press CTRL + C	To create a copy of the selected shape.

5 Press [CTRL] + [V]   A copy of the shape appears in the middle of the Stage.

6 Point to the copy

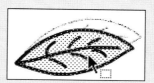

   Drag the copy below the original leaf

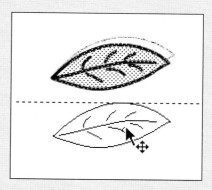

   Deselect the leaf

7 Create another copy of the leaf   Press Ctrl+V again.

   Drag the third copy underneath the chili drawing on the left

8 Select the original leaf   You'll delete the image of this leaf.

9 Press [DELETE]   The shape is deleted from the Stage.

10 Save your changes

Creating groups

You can group shapes to perform shared actions on them, such as copying, moving, or applying color. To create a group, select the shapes that you want to include in the group and then choose Modify, Group. A blue rectangle appears around the shapes, indicating that they are grouped. To ungroup shapes, select the group and choose Modify, Ungroup.

You can modify a group as well as the shapes that constitute a group. To modify a group, double-click the group and make the desired modifications. When you double-click the group, the images that are not included in the group appear faded. This indicates that the group is in Edit mode. To deselect a group, double-click anywhere on the Stage or press Esc. To modify an individual shape in the group, select the group, then select the shape, and make your desired modifications.

B-4: Grouping objects

Here's how	Here's why
1 Select the two leaves	Use the Selection tool.
2 Choose **Modify, Group**	
	To group the shapes. A blue outline appears around the selected leaves, indicating that they are grouped.
3 Using the Selection tool, double-click either leaf	Both leaves are selected.
4 Move the leaves to another location on the Stage	The leaves move as one.
Deselect the group	Press Esc or click anywhere on the Stage.
5 Click either leaf	The blue line re-appears, indicating that the two leaves are a group.
6 Choose **Modify, Ungroup**	To ungroup the leaves.
Deselect the leaves	
7 Save and close the document	

Unit summary: Shapes

Topic A   In this topic, you learned how to create basic shapes such as rectangles, squares, ovals, and circles by using the Rectangle and Oval tools. You also learned how to use **rulers** to create precise shape sizes. Finally, you learned how to create **freeform shapes**.

Topic B   In this topic, you learned how to use the Selection, Subselection, and Lasso tools. Then, you learned how to change line styles, **transform shapes**, and copy, move, and delete a shape. Finally, you learned how to **group** shapes.

Independent practice activity

1 Open Shapes practice.fla from the current unit folder.

2 Save the file as **My Shapes practice** in the current unit folder.

3 Change the magnification to **Fit in Window**.

4 Create four copies of the leaf. (*Hint*: Move each leaf from the center of the Stage.)

5 Set the fill color to a shade of blue.

6 Use the Oval tool to draw an oval big enough to include all five leaves.

7 Use the Pencil tool to create the shape of a small branch or stem.

8 Rotate and position the branch and the leaves to create a drawing similar to the one shown in Exhibit 2-4.

9 Save and close the document. Don't close Flash.

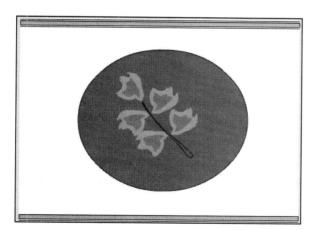

Exhibit 2-4: A small branch with leaves

Unit 3

Color

Unit time: 50 minutes

Complete this unit, and you'll know how to:

A Use the Paint Bucket and Ink Bottle tools to apply fill and stroke colors, copy an existing color for re-use in a document, and apply different brush styles.

B Use the Color Mixer to create and save a custom color, create linear and radial gradients, customize gradient colors, and save a custom gradient.

Topic A: Applying color

Explanation

A shape can have several properties, including various stroke styles, stroke colors, and fill colors. To apply a stroke or fill color to a shape, first you need to select the color from the Colors section of the Toolbox. Then, you can use tools like the Paint Bucket, Ink Bottle, Eyedropper, or Brush to apply the color.

The Colors section

The Colors section of the Toolbox contains the Stroke Color and Fill Color boxes. The three buttons under them, shown in Exhibit 3-1, help you to modify the color settings of your shapes.

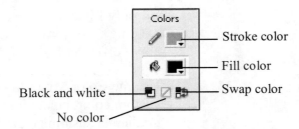

Exhibit 3-1: The Colors section

When you create a new shape, it will have the stroke and fill colors that you last selected from the Fill and Stroke color palettes.

The options in the Colors section of the Tools panel allow you to:

- **Specify the stroke color of a shape**. Select a shape, click the Stroke Color box to display the Stroke color palette, and select the desired stroke color.

- **Specify the fill color of a shape**. Select a shape, click the Fill Color box to display the Fill Color palette, and select the desired fill color.

- **Swap the fill and stroke colors**. Click the Swap Colors button in the lower-right corner of the Colors section to toggle between the fill and stroke colors of the selected shape.

- **Revert to the default colors**. Click the Black and White button in the lower-left corner of the Colors section to change the stroke color to black and the fill color to white.

- **Create a shape with no fill or stroke color**. When you are creating a new shape, click the No color button to create a shape with no fill or stroke color. You can't use the No color button to modify an existing shape.

The colors in the color palette appear in the form of tiles called *swatches*. To apply a color to a shape, select a swatch from the color palette or specify the hexadecimal value for the color in the palette.

Hexadecimal values

Hexadecimal values are based on the base 16 number system. The sequence of numbers in this number system is 0-9, followed by letters from A-F. The numbers 0-9 represent the first 10 numbers in the decimal number system, and A-F represent numbers from 10-15. By combining these values into a six-character code, you can specify millions of different colors.

Hexadecimal values correspond to Red, Green, Blue (RGB) values. A hexadecimal value begins with the pound sign (#) followed by six numbers (0-9) or characters (A-F). The first two values in the six-character sequence refer to the intensity of red in the color. The second two values indicate the intensity of green in the color, and the last two values represent the intensity of blue in the color. The range of values is 00 through FF. A value of 00 indicates no value for a red, green, or blue value. The letters FF indicate full intensity of red, green, or blue. The color that results is a combination of all these red, green, and blue values. The following table shows some commonly used colors and their hexadecimal values.

Color	Value and description
Black	#000000 (No red, green, or blue values)
White	#FFFFFF (Full intensity of red, green, and blue values)
Red	#FF0000 (Only red)
Yellow	#FFFF00 (Full intensity of red and green)
Green	#00FF00 (Only green)
Blue	#0000FF (Only blue)

Gradient swatches

The Fill Color box also contains gradient swatches. A *gradient* is a smooth transition between two or more colors, where one color blends into another. You can apply gradients to fills, but you cannot apply a gradient to a stroke.

The Paint Bucket tool

You use the Paint Bucket tool to apply fill color to a shape. To use this tool:

1 Select it, and then select the desired option from the Options section.
2 From the Fill Color palette, select a color.
3 Click inside the shape to which you want to apply the fill color.

When you select the Paint Bucket tool, two modifiers appear in the Options section, Gap Size and Lock Fill. The Gap Size modifier adds color to a shape that is not closed and has small gaps. When you click this modifier, a list appears containing various options for the gap size. These options help you to add color to a shape, depending on the size of the gap between the start and end points of the shape. The Lock Fill modifier adds gradient color to a shape in such a way that the gradient color appears to be stretched across the shape.

The Ink Bottle tool

You use the Ink Bottle tool to apply stroke color to a shape. To use this tool:

1 Select it.
2 In the Colors section of the Toolbox, click the Stroke Color button down-arrow to display the Stroke Color palette, and then select the color of your choice.
3 Click the shape to which you want to apply the stroke color.

Do it!

A-1: Using the Paint Bucket and Ink Bottle tools

Here's how	Here's why
1 Open Colors.fla	(From the current unit folder.) This file contains various shapes that you'll modify.
2 Save the file as **MyColors** Hide any open panels	In the current unit folder.
3 Change the zoom setting to **Fit in Window**	To display the entire Stage on the screen.
4 Click	To activate the Paint Bucket tool. You will change the fill color of shapes.
5 Click the Fill Color box	 (In the Colors section.) To display the Fill Color palette.

6 Select the red swatch, as shown

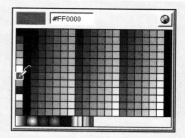

The hexadecimal value for red (#FF0000) is displayed at the top of the palette.

7 Click between the two outer strokes

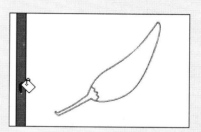

8 In the Fill Color palette, enter **00cc00**

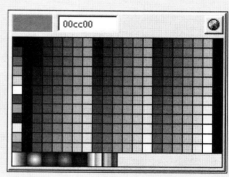

Press (↵ ENTER)

9 Fill the leaf with this color

(Click inside it.) The fill color is applied to the leaf shape.

10 Click

To activate the Ink Bottle tool. You will change the color of the stroke.

11 Under the Colors section, click the Stroke Color box

To display the Stroke Color palette.

12 In the color palette, enter **0030ce**

    Press ⏎ ENTER

This is the hexadecimal value for a shade of blue.

13 Click inside the oval

The stroke color of the oval changes to blue.

14 Activate the Selection tool

15 Double click the stroke of the rectangle

You'll change the stroke color of this shape.

16 Activate the Ink Bottle tool

    From the Stroke Color palette, select a color of your choice

The rectangle's stroke color changes accordingly.

17 From the Fill Color palette, select a color of your choice

18 Activate the Paint Bucket tool

    Click inside the rectangle

The fill color of the rectangle changes accordingly.

    Deselect the shape

19 Save your changes

The Eyedropper and Brush tools

You use the Eyedropper tool to copy an existing stroke or fill color and apply it to another stroke or shape. To use the Eyedropper tool to copy a stroke color:

1 Select the tool and point to the stroke whose color you want to copy. The pointer changes to an eyedropper and a pencil.
2 Click the stroke. The pointer changes to an ink bottle.
3 Click the stroke to which you want to apply the copied color.

To use the Eyedropper tool to copy a fill color:

1 Select the Eyedropper tool and point to the fill color you want to copy. The pointer changes to an eyedropper and a paintbrush.
2 Click the fill color. The pointer changes to a paint bucket.
3 Click inside the shape to which you want to apply the fill color.

The Brush tool is used to add brush-like strokes to an image, as shown in Exhibit 3-2. After you select the Brush tool, you can change its size and shape by selecting options from the various modifiers that appear in the Options section of the Toolbox, shown in Exhibit 3-3.

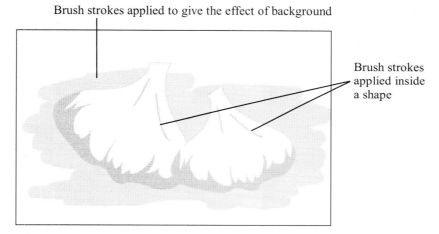

Exhibit 3-2: The use of the Brush tool to add special effects to an image

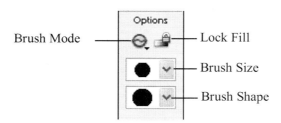

Exhibit 3-3: The modifiers for the Brush tool

The Brush Size modifier specifies the size of the brush while the Brush Shape specifies its shape. The function of the Lock Fill modifier is to create the appearance of a gradient fill over multiple shapes. The Brush Mode modifier has various options, which are described in the following table.

Option	Description
Paint Normal	The brush strokes will appear above all other strokes or fills in the area or shape.
Paint Fills	The brush strokes will appear only above the existing fill color of a shape, and can only paint a fill color. It will not affect strokes.
Paint Behind	The brush strokes will apply only to the background of the area or shape.
Paint Inside	The brush strokes will apply only to the selected area(s).

Do it!

A-2:   Using the Eyedropper and Brush tools

Here's how	Here's why
1 Click	To activate the Eyedropper tool.
Change the magnification to **100%**	
2 Point to the red boundary you created earlier	A paintbrush appears under the Eyedropper. This indicates that clicking will select the fill color.
3 Click the red boundary	The pointer changes to a paint bucket with a lock. This indicates that a color is "locked in," and you can apply this locked in color to other areas on the Stage.
Observe the Toolbox	The Paint Bucket tool is now selected.

4 Click inside both chili drawings

The images are filled with the same red color that you copied.

5 Fill the stems of both chilies with the green leaf color

Use the Eyedropper tool to copy the color and the Paint Bucket tool to apply the color.

6 Activate the Eyedropper tool

If necessary.

Point to the oval stroke

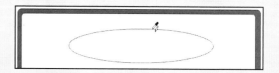

A pencil appears under the eyedropper. This indicates that clicking will select the stroke color.

7 Click the stroke of the oval

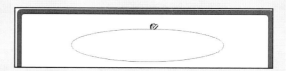

The pointer changes to an ink bottle. The stroke color is copied.

Observe the Toolbox

The Eyedropper tool is no longer selected. The Ink Bottle tool is now selected.

Click the rectangle stroke

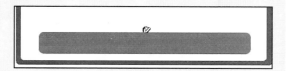

The stroke of the rectangle changes to blue.

8 Click [brush icon]

To activate the Brush tool. The pointer changes to a black circle.

Change the fill color to **00CC00**

If necessary.

9 In the Options section, click   To display the Brush Mode list.

Select **Paint Fills**   You'll paint only the fills, without affecting the outline.

From the Brush Size list, select the smallest size

From the Brush Shape list, select the second diagonal shape, as shown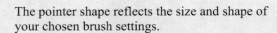

10 Point to one of the chilis   The pointer shape reflects the size and shape of your chosen brush settings.

11 Click and drag as shown

Apply similar brush strokes to the other chili

12 Save your changes

Topic B: Custom colors and gradients

Explanation

You're not limited to the colors and gradients that appear in the Fill Color or Stroke Color palettes. You can create your own custom colors and gradients and save them for later use. You can also create Stroke styles with specific attributes, such as thickness and color, which are not available by default.

Custom colors and color modes

Flash makes it easy to create custom colors that you can apply to any object. A *color mode* defines the process by which colors are specified. There are three color modes in Flash: RGB, HSB, and Hex, as described in the following table.

Mode	Description
RGB	RGB colors are known as additive colors because you mix them to achieve a desired color. RGB values range from 0 to 255, where 0 represents no red, green, or blue value, and 255 represents full intensity of red, green, or blue. Therefore, an RGB value of 0,0,0 represents black, while a value of 255,255,255 represents white.
HSB (Hue, Saturation, Brightness)	Based on the way we perceive colors, according to the hue, intensity, and purity of that color (saturation), and its luminosity (brightness).
Hex (Hexadecimal)	A code of six alphanumeric characters from 0 through 9 and A through F, whose value pairs correspond to RGB values.

The Color Mixer

You can use the Color Mixer to create a custom color.

To create a custom color:

1   Select a color from the Fill Color or Stroke Color palette. You can also select a color from the Color selector bar in the Color Mixer.

2   From the Options menu, select a color mode. Depending on the selected color mode, the values in the R, G, B, and Alpha boxes change.

3   Enter values in the R, G, and B boxes to create a custom color.

4   Enter a value in the Alpha box to specify a level of transparency, if desired.

5   From the Options menu, choose Add Swatch. The color is saved in either the Fill Color or Stroke Color palette depending on which one you had selected.

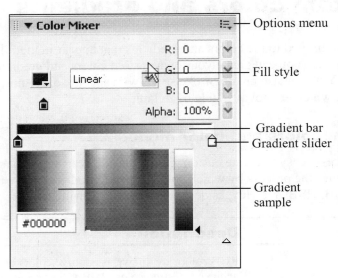

Exhibit 3-4: The Color Mixer

Do it!

B-1: Creating a custom color swatch

Here's how	Here's why
1 Activate the Selection tool Select the leaf	 The leaf appears dotted, indicating that it's selected.
2 Choose **Window**, **Design Panels**, **Color Mixer**	To display the Color Mixer, as shown in Exhibit 3-4.
3 In the Color Mixer panel, click the Fill Color box	 To display the Fill Color palette.
4 Change the color to **996633** Press (← ENTER) Observe the values in the R, G, and B boxes	 The leaf changes to a shade of brown. They correspond to the intensity values of red, green, and blue, respectively. Hexadecimal values are a way to express these RGB values.
5 Observe the value in the Alpha box	The Alpha value indicates the level of transparency for the selected color. A value of 0% represents complete transparency, and a value of 100% represents complete opacity.

6 Click the down-arrow next to the R box as indicated

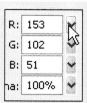

To display the red value slider.

Drag the slider downwards to 132 as shown

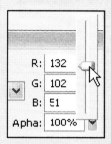

Click anywhere in the Color Mixer panel

To close the red value slider.

7 Set the G value to **113**

Display the green value slider and drag it so that the value in the G box reads 113. Click anywhere in the Mixer panel to close the slider.

8 In the B box, enter **125**

To manually enter a blue value.

9 Change the Alpha value to **56%**

(Drag the slider downwards or enter the value manually.) To change the transparency for this color.

Click anywhere in the Color Mixer

To close the Alpha value slider.

10 In the Color Mixer, click the Options menu icon, as shown

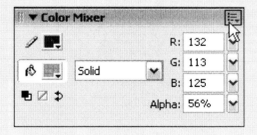

To display the Options menu.

Choose **Add Swatch**

To save your custom color.

Click anywhere on the Stage

To deselect the leaf. The new color is applied to the leaf.

11 Save your changes

Gradient fills

Explanation

You can use the Color Mixer panel to apply gradient fills. A gradient is a transition from one color to another. There are two types of gradients, Linear and Radial. In Linear gradients, the transition of colors is linear across a shape. In Radial, the transition of colors occurs in a circular form. The starting color for the gradient appears in the center of the circular gradient and transitions outward.

Do it!

B-2: Applying gradients

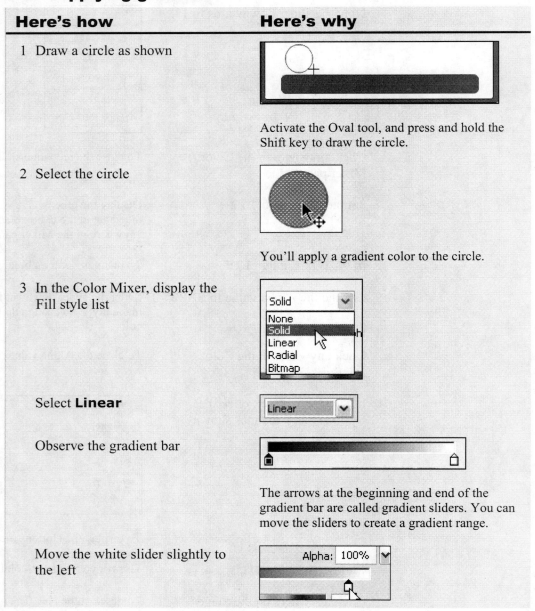

Here's how	Here's why
1 Draw a circle as shown	Activate the Oval tool, and press and hold the Shift key to draw the circle.
2 Select the circle	You'll apply a gradient color to the circle.
3 In the Color Mixer, display the Fill style list	
Select **Linear**	
Observe the gradient bar	The arrows at the beginning and end of the gradient bar are called gradient sliders. You can move the sliders to create a gradient range.
Move the white slider slightly to the left	

4 Move the black slider slightly to
the right

Observe the gradient sample box

To preview the gradient.

5 Deselect the circle

The fill color appears with the black-to-white
gradient.

6 Select the circle again

Use the R, G, and B sliders to
change the gradient color

Deselect the circle

7 Save your changes

Custom gradients

Explanation

To create a custom gradient:

1 On the Color Mixer, from the Fill style list, select a gradient type.

2 The gradient bar, gradient slider, and the gradient preview box appear below the Fill style list. You can adjust the position of the various sliders by moving them. As you move the sliders, a new gradient is created and a preview of it appears in the Gradient sample box.

3 Display the Options menu and choose Add Swatch. The gradient is added to the Fill Color palette.

Do it!

B-3:   Creating a custom gradient

Here's how	Here's why
1 Select the circle	You'll create a new gradient style and color.
2 From the Fill style list, select **Radial**	The gradient style changes.
3 Click the leftmost gradient slider	To select the start of the gradient. You will change the color for the beginning of the gradient.
4 Display the Fill Color palette	
Change the gradient color to **FF9900** as shown	
Press (↵ ENTER)	

5 Observe the gradient bar

The new color gradient appears.

6 In the gradient bar, click as shown

A new slider appears where you clicked.

In the Hexadecimal code box, enter **FF0000**

To specify a new gradient color.

Press (↵ ENTER)

#FF0000

The new gradient color appears.

Observe the gradient bar

7 Click the rightmost gradient slider

Change the gradient color to **FFFF66**

To set the ending gradient color to a shade of yellow.

Observe the gradient bar

Observe the changes to the circle

The gradient color begins at orange, transitions to red, and ends in a shade of yellow.

8 Display the Options menu

Click the down-arrow in the upper-right corner of the Color Mixer panel.

Choose **Add Swatch**

To save the custom gradient in the Fill Color palette.

Deselect the circle

9   Observe the Colors section of the Toolbox

The custom gradient appears in the Fill Color box.

10 Display the Fill Color palette

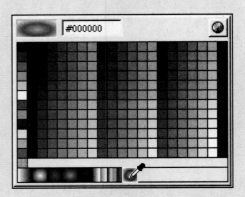

The custom gradient appears as a predefined option at the bottom of the palette.

11 Save and close the document

Unit summary: Color

Topic A   In this topic, you learned how to use the **Fill Color** and **Stroke Color** boxes. You also learned how to use the Paint Bucket and Ink Bottle tools to apply fill and stroke colors. Then, you learned how to copy an existing color for re-use in a document, and apply different **brush styles**.

Topic B   In this topic, you learned how to use the **Color Mixer** to create and save a custom color, create **linear** and **radial gradients**, customize gradient colors, and save a custom gradient.

Independent practice activity

1 Open Colors practice.fla.

2 Save the file as **My Colors practice** in the current unit folder.

3 Fill the area around the edge of the Stage with a color or gradient of your choice.

4 In the drawing of the three circles, fill each circle with a different color. Apply one stroke color to the stroke of all three circles.

5 Fill the flower and chef drawings with colors of your choice.

6 Display the Color Mixer panel.

7 Create a new Linear gradient with four different colors.

8 Save this gradient as a swatch.

9 Use the gradient to fill the area between the pointed lines and the upper-left border of the Stage.

10 Activate the Brush tool. From the Brush Mode list, select **Paint Behind**. Change the brush size to a larger size and the brush shape to an oval style.

11 Apply brush strokes behind the chef drawing.

12 Close the Color Mixer panel.

13 Save and close the document. Don't close Flash.

Unit 4

Text

Unit time: 50 minutes

Complete this unit, and you'll know how to:

A Create text blocks, change the font face, font size, and color of text, and move text blocks on the Stage.

B Format, skew, scale, and align text, create aliased text, adjust the spacing between lines and characters, and set margins and indentation.

C Use the Find and Replace feature, the Spell Checker, and the History panel.

Topic A: The Text tool

Explanation

You can add text in a Flash document by using the Text tool. The Text tool creates a rectangle, called a *text block,* in which you type your text. You can create three types of text blocks: extending, fixed, and scrollable. You can also convert one type of text block to another. Text in a text block is also considered static, meaning it does not change.

Extending text blocks

Explanation

Flash uses the *extended text block* to insert short lines of text, such as titles or captions. You identify an extending text block by the circle in its upper-right corner, as shown in Exhibit 4-1.

To create an extending text block:

1   Select the Text tool.
2   Click the Stage.
3   Type your text.

The text block will expand horizontally as you type. By default, text appears in a single line on the Stage, and if the line of text is longer than the stage, the text will continue off the Stage and into the work area. To start a new line in an extending text block, press Enter.

Exhibit 4-1: An extending text block

After you have entered text, you can select it with the Selection tool and then apply font and color styles by using the Property inspector or the Text menu. By default, Flash inserts text with the font Times New Roman and a font size of 12 pixels.

Do it!   **A-1:   Creating an extending text block**

Here's how	**Here's why**
1 Open Text.fla	From the current unit folder.
2 Save the file as **MyText**	In the current unit folder.
3 Click ![A]	To activate the Text tool. The pointer changes to a plus sign with the letter A.
4 Click the area above the image	 (Scroll up if necessary.) A rectangle appears with an insertion point and a circle on its upper-right corner. This is an extending text block, which is best used for short lines of text such as titles or captions.
5 Type **Outlander Spices**	 As you type, the text block extends to fit the text.
6 Activate the Selection tool	 The text is surrounded by a blue border, which indicates that the entire text block is selected.
Display the Property inspector	 These are the default text styles that Flash applies to a document.

7 Click the font size down-arrow

To display the Font Size slider. You'll increase the size of the selected text by using the slider.

Drag the slider upwards until the value in the box reads **28**

To change the font size of the selected text block to 28 pixels. Note that the text size changes along with the slider's value.

Click anywhere in the Property inspector

(If necessary.) To close the slider.

8 Click the Text color box

(On the Property inspector.) To display the Text color palette.

Select a dark red color

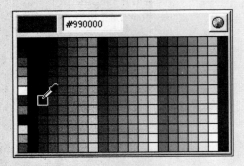

To change the text color.

9 Activate the Font list

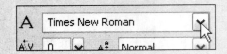

(On the Property inspector, click the down-arrow shown here.) To display a list of several different font faces.

Scroll up and select **Arial**

To apply the font face Arial to this text.

10 Save and close the document

Fixed text blocks

Explanation

You can use a *fixed text block* to insert large blocks of text in a document. To create a fixed text block, you first create a frame. A *frame* is a boundary that encloses the text. As you type text in a fixed text block, it wraps to the next line when it reaches the right edge of the frame, and the frame will increase in height if you enter more text than the drawn height will allow.

To create a fixed text block, use the Text tool and drag horizontally to define the dimensions of a text frame. A square appears on the upper-right corner of the text block, as shown in Exhibit 4-2. This indicates that it's a fixed text block. You can resize a fixed text block by dragging this square.

Exhibit 4-2: A fixed text block

You convert a fixed text block into an extending text block by double-clicking the square on the upper-right corner. To convert an extending text block to a fixed text block, drag the circle in its upper-right corner in any direction.

Moving a text block

After you create a text block, you move it by pointing to the boundary of the text block and dragging it to the desired location. When you move a text block, a dotted outline of the text block appears and follows your pointer, as shown in Exhibit 4-3. When you release the mouse button, the text block will appear in the new location.

Exhibit 4-3: Moving a text block

Do it!

A-2: Creating a fixed text block

Here's how	Here's why
1 Open Home.fla	
2 Save the file as **MyHome**	In the current unit folder.
3 Activate the Text tool	You'll create a fixed text block.
In the Property inspector, verify that the font face is set to **Arial** and the color is dark red	
Set the font size to **13**	
4 Point to just below the text **Welcome to Outlander Spices** as shown	
5 Drag to the end of the gray dotted line	
	When you release the mouse button, a text block appears.
6 Move the text block slightly downward as shown	
7 Type **We bring you a rich heritage of the finest spices from all over the world. You can find our kiosks in grocery and specialty stores all over the country, or you can order directly from this Web site.**	
8 Activate the Selection tool	
9 Change the text color to black	
Save your changes	

Topic B: Text formatting

Explanation

There are many ways to format text. You have already changed the font face, size, and color by using the Property inspector. You can also set text as bold or italic, control text alignment, apply margins, adjust the spacing between letters, and convert text characters to vector graphics to use them as shapes.

Applying text styles

Before you can apply styles to text, you need to select the text. You can use the Selection tool to apply styles to all the text in a text block, or you can use the Text tool to apply styles to specific letters or words in a text block.

To select specific letters or words in a text block:

- Select the Text tool.
- Click and drag to select a specific letter, word, or phrase in the text block.

Bold and italic text

The two most common font styles are bold and italic. To create bold or italic text, click the Bold or Italic button on the Property inspector. You can also choose Text, Style, and choose an option from the submenu.

B-1:   Changing font styles

Here's how	Here's why
1 Click as shown	 (Scroll up if necessary.) To select the entire text block.
2 Click **B**	(On the Property inspector.) To apply bold formatting to the selected text.
3 Deselect the text	 The text appears bold.
4 Save your changes	
5 Activate the Text tool	
Select the text **rich heritage of the finest spices**	
6 Make the selected text bold	
7 Select the entire paragraph	
Click *I*	(On the Property inspector.) To make the selected text italic.
8 Deselect the text	 The paragraph text is italic, and some of the text is bold.
Save your changes	

Skewing, scaling, and aligning text

Explanation

You can change the size of a text block by using the Scale modifier of the Free Transform tool. When you re-size a text block with this tool, the size of the text block increases or decreases, as well as the text inside that text block. To resize a text block by using the Free Transform tool:

1 Select the text block.

2 Activate the Free Transform tool.

3 Use the Scale modifier to increase or decrease the size of the text block.

You can also rotate and skew a text block by using the Rotate and Skew modifier.

Aligning text

You can align text to the left, right, or center of a text block. You can also justify text, which means that the text will be flush against the left and right sides of its text block. To achieve a justified alignment, spaces are typically added between words, and these spaces are usually not uniform in length. You change alignments in two ways. You can choose Text, Align, and then choose an alignment option from the submenu. Or you can select the text block, and click the desired alignment button in the Property inspector.

Do it!

B-2: Modifying a text block

Here's how	Here's why
1 Activate the Selection tool	
2 Select the paragraph text block	Welcome to Outlander Spices *We bring you a **rich heritage of the fines** can find our kiosks in grocery and special can order directly from this Web site.* (If necessary.) You'll change the alignment of text in this text block.
3 In the Property inspector, observe the alignment buttons	The Align Left button is selected, indicating the current and default alignment of text.
4 Click [center icon]	The text is centered in its block.
5 Click [justify icon]	The text is justified in its block.
6 Select the heading text block	Welcome to Outlander Spices *We bring you a **rich heritage of the fine*** You'll skew and scale this text block.
7 Activate the Free Transform tool	Welcome to Outlander Spices *We bring you a **rich heritage of the fines*** *can find our kiosks in grocery and special*
8 Choose **Window**, **Design Panels**, **Transform**	▼ Transform ↔ 100.0% ↕ 100.0% ☐ Constrain ⊙ Rotate △ 0.0° ○ Skew 0.0° 0.0° To open the Transform dialog box.

9   Verify that the Width setting is **100.0%**

In the Height box, enter **150.0%**

To scale the height of the text.

10 Select **Skew**

You'll skew the text.

In the Skew horizontally box, enter **20**

⊙ Skew   🖉 20°   ◹ 0.0°

Press [⏎ ENTER]

Close the Transform dialog box

Welcome to Ostlander Spices

The height of the text block increases, and it appears slanted to the right.

11 Save your changes

Aliased and anti-aliased text

Explanation

When you create text in Flash, the text is anti-aliased by default. *Anti-aliasing* smooths over the jagged edges between solid colors by introducing intermediate colors to create a "blending" effect. As a result, anti-aliased text characters and shapes appear smoother to the eye, as shown in Exhibit 4-4. However, because anti-aliased text has more intermediate colors, it can be more difficult to read the text at very small sizes. Therefore, whenever you create text that you intend to be small, consider using the Alias Text button to disable anti-aliasing for that text.

Exhibit 4-4: A close-up of anti-aliased text (left) and aliased text (right)

Do it!

B-3:   Aliasing small text

Here's how	Here's why
1 Activate the Selection tool	
2 Select the text block at the bottom of the page	
	Note that the text appears blurry at this small font size.
3 Zoom in on this text block	(Activate the Zoom tool and then click the text.) Note that the text appears smooth at any level of magnification. This is because the text is anti-aliased.
4 From the Zoom list, select **100%**	100%
	(In the upper-right corner of the document window.) To return to the original magnification.
5 Click [A]	(On the Property inspector.) To put this text in aliased mode.
Deselect the text block	The text is now easier to read at this font size.
6 Zoom in on the text	
	When magnified, the text appears choppy because there are no intermediate colors to create the illusion of rounded edges.
From the Zoom list, select **100%**	
7 Save your changes	

Setting character spacing and kerning

Explanation

Kerning is the space between letters. It's also referred to as character spacing or letter spacing. Most fonts have their own built-in kerning settings, which is why some fonts appear to have more space between individual letters than other fonts. You use the Character spacing box to adjust the kerning of letters in a text block. First, select the text block, and then enter a value in the Character spacing box or use the slider to set the character spacing for the text block.

Do it!

B-4: Adjusting the kerning of text

Here's how	Here's why
1 Select the welcome text as shown	
2 In the Character Spacing box, enter **3**	(On the Property inspector.) To increase the spacing between letters in this text block by 3 pixels.
Press ⏎ ENTER	The spacing between each letter increases.
3 Increase the kerning of the topmost text to 4 as shown	
4 Save your changes	

Line spacing, margins, and indentation

From the Property inspector, you can also control the space between adjacent lines of text, which is also called *leading*, and you can set margins and indentation. Margins are the space on the left and right side of a text block. Indentation is the amount of space that the first line of text in a paragraph is offset from its normal starting point.

To set line spacing, margins, and indentation, select the text block you want to modify and then click the Format button on the Property inspector. The Format Options dialog box opens, as shown in Exhibit 4-5. The default line spacing for a text block is 2 pt (points), which depends upon the font choice in use.

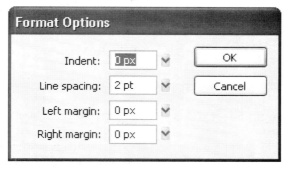

Exhibit 4-5: The Format Options dialog box

B-5: Setting line spacing, margins, and indentation

Here's how	Here's why
1 Select the paragraph	(Starting with "We bring you.") You will change the formatting of this paragraph.
2 Click **Format**	[Format...]
	(On the Property inspector.) To open the Format Options dialog box.
3 In the Indent box, enter **20**	To increase the indentation.
4 In the Line spacing box, enter **5**	To increase the line spacing.
5 In the Left margin box, enter **8**	To increase the left margin on the text box.
6 In the Right margin box, enter **8**	To increase the right margin by the same amount.
7 Click **OK**	To apply your changes.
Verify the results	*Welcome to Outlander Spices* **We bring you a rich heritage of the finest spices** from all over the world. You can find our kiosks in grocery and specialty stores all over the country, or you can order directly from this Web site.
	The space between the lines of text increases, the first line is indented, and there's a small margin on both sides of the text block.
8 Save and close the document	

Topic C: Text utilities

Explanation

Flash MX 2004 provides several utilities to increase your productivity, including a Find and Replace feature, a spelling checker, and a History Panel to record and track your changes to a document.

Find and Replace

By using the Find and Replace dialog box, shown in Exhibit 4-6, you can search for a word or text string, a font type, a color, and other document objects. To open the Find and Replace dialog box, choose Edit, Find and Replace, or press Ctrl+F3.

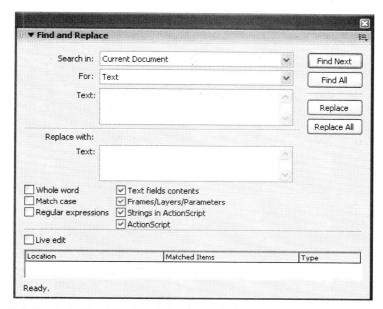

Exhibit 4-6: The Find and Replace dialog box

In the For list, you specify the element type you want to search for. The default selection is Text. When you search for text, there are several options you can choose from to make your search more specific. For example, use the Whole word option to search for complete words rather than parts of words, and use the Match case option to search for case-sensitive terms.

C-1: Using the Find and Replace feature

Here's how	Here's why
1 Open Homepage.fla	
2 Save the file as **MyHomepage**	
3 In the first paragraph, locate the word "site"	You will replace this text with the words "Web site."
4 Choose **Edit**, **Find and Replace**	To open the Find and Replace dialog box.
5 In the Text box, enter **site**	Text: site
	You will search the document for this word.
6 In the Replace with box, enter **Web site**	Replace with: Text: Web site
	The text will replace the search text.
7 Check **Whole word**	You'll search for instances of the complete word, rather than words of which it is a part.
8 Check **Match case**	So that Flash will match the case of the specified word. If the word Site appears with a capital S, it will not be found in this search.
9 Click **Replace**	The detail of the replaced word appears at the bottom of the dialog box.
10 Close the dialog box	
Observe the text on the Stage	grocery and speci this Web site. W variety.
	The text "Web site" replaced the text "site."
11 Save your changes	

The Spell Checker

Explanation

You can use the Spell Checker feature to search a document for spelling errors. Choose Text, Check Spelling to open the Check Spelling dialog box, as shown in Exhibit 4-7.

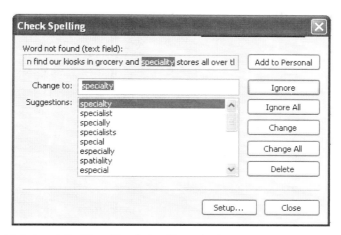

Exhibit 4-7: The Check Spelling dialog box

When the spelling checker finds a word that's not in its dictionary, it appears highlighted in the Word not found box. You can take several different actions on a word that's found by the spelling checker.

- If the word is acceptable and you want to add it to your personal dictionary so that it's not considered a spelling error in the future, click the Add to Personal button.

- If the word is acceptable but you don't want to add the word to your personal dictionary, click the Ignore button to leave the word unchanged.

- Click the Ignore All button to leave all the instances of a word unchanged.

- Click the Change button if the word that's selected in the Suggestions box is the correct word.

- Click the Delete button to delete the word from the document.

- Click the Setup button to change your Spelling options.

C-2:   Using the Spell Checker feature

Here's how	Here's why
1 Choose **Text**, **Check Spelling...**	To open the Check Spelling dialog box, which begins searching the document for incorrectly spelled words or any words that do not exist in the Flash dictionary.
Observe the results	The word "speciality" appears in the Word not found (text field) box.
2 Observe the Change to box	Change to: specialty / Suggestions: specialty, specialist
	The word "specialty" is selected by default. This is the correct spelling of the word.
3 Click **Change**	To replace the misspelled word with the correct spelling of the word.
Observe the dialog box	The Spell Checker shows that another word is found.
4 Click **Change**	To change the word "Yoghurt" to "Yogurt."
Observe the dialog box	The Spell Checker shows that another word is found.
5 Click **Ignore All**	To ignore all instances of the found word.
6 Click **Change All**	To change all instances of the word "chilli" with "chili." A message appears indicating that the Spell Checker has reached the end of the document.
Click **Yes**	To continue to check the document, in case the checker started at a point other than the beginning of the document. A message appears indicating that the spelling check is complete.
Click **OK**	To close the message box.
7 Save your changes	

The History panel

When you work on a document, you might want to perform an action repeatedly or undo unwanted actions. The History panel records every action you take on a document, and allows you to repeat or undo single actions or a series of actions. To open the History panel, choose Windows, Other Panels, History, or press Ctrl+F10.

The History panel contains a slider, which initially points to the last step that you performed. To specify the number of actions you want to undo, drag the slider. When you undo a step, the step appears disabled in the History panel. You can also click the Replay button to redo an action. To clear the steps from the History panel, choose Clear History from the History panel options menu.

Do it!

C-3: Using the History panel

Here's how	Here's why
1 Choose **Window**, **Other Panels**, **History**	To display the History panel.
2 Observe the History panel	
3 Point to the slider on the left side of the panel	
	You'll drag the slider upwards to undo your recent changes.
4 Drag the slider up two actions	
Observe the changes on the Stage	The word "chili" reverts to the incorrectly spelled "chilli."
5 Drag the slider back down	To redo the changes you had made to the document.
6 Close the History panel	
7 Save your changes and close the document	

Unit summary: Text

Topic A

In this topic, you learned how to create **extending** and **fixed text blocks**. You learned how to move and resize text blocks. Then, you learned how to use the **Property inspector** to change the font face, font size, and color of text.

Topic B

In this topic, you learned how to use the Property inspector to create bold and italic text. Then, you learned how to **skew**, **scale**, and **align** text, and create **aliased** text. Finally, you learned how to adjust the space between characters, the space between adjacent lines of text, and you learned how to apply **margins** and **indentation**.

Topic C

In this topic, you learned how use the Find and Replace feature, the Spell Checker, and the **History panel**.

Independent practice activity

1 From the current unit folder, open Practice.fla.

2 Save the file as **MyPractice** in the current unit folder.

3 At the top of the document, change the color of the text "Outlander Spices" to **#990000**.

4 Move the text **Welcome to Outlander Spices** so that the W is lined up with the left edge of the image above it, about half an inch below.

5 Add four extending text blocks next to the circles along the left side of the document, as shown in Exhibit 4-8. In the first text block, type **About Us**. In the second text block, type **Locations**. In the third text block, type **Products**. In the last text block, type **Feedback**. Give these text blocks the same text styles as the "Home" text.

6 Create a fixed text block between the two chilies, with the text **Recipe of the Day**. Make the color of this text the same as the "Welcome to Outlander Spices" text.

7 Set the kerning (character spacing) of the "Recipe of the Day" text to **4**.

8 Move the text block with the paragraphs so that it lines up below the "Welcome to Outlander Spices" text. Give this text a different font of your choice, and make it **black** with a font size of **13**. Justify and alias the text. Increase the kerning of this text block to **1**, and set its line spacing to **4 pts**.

9 Compare your results with Exhibit 4-8.

10 Save your changes and close the document. Don't close Flash.

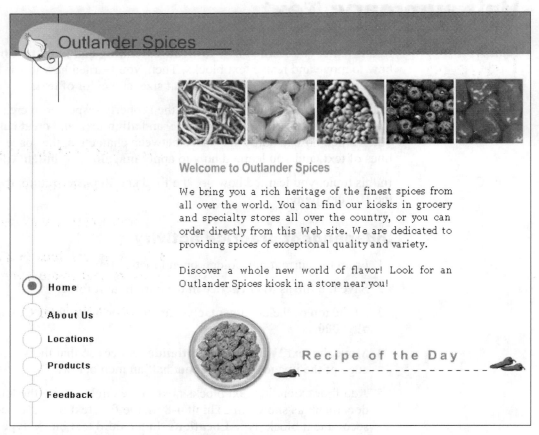

Exhibit 4-8: The completed document

Unit 5

Layers

Unit time: 40 minutes

Complete this unit, and you'll know how to:

A Create, merge, rearrange, and delete layers.

B Name layers, lock or hide layers, mask layers, and create layer folders.

C Create a guide layer.

Topic A: Layer basics

Explanation   Layers are like transparent sheets of paper stacked on top of each other. *Layers* help you create, edit, and organize the objects and content in your Flash documents. You can have different elements of an image on different layers and then combine these layers to form a composite image. For example, if you have an image of an apple on one layer and a plate on another layer, you can stack the two layers to create the image of an apple on a plate. The advantage of using different layers is that you can edit specific areas of an image without affecting other shapes and images.

The Layers list

You use the Layers list in the Timeline panel, shown in Exhibit 5-1, to create and name layers. The Layers list contains the names of all the layers in a document, and they're arranged according to their sequence in the document. When you create a new Flash document, it contains one layer, named Layer 1, by default.

You can make changes to only one layer at a time. The selected layer is highlighted in the Layers list, and a pencil icon appears next to the layer name. In Exhibit 5-1, the images layer is the selected layer.

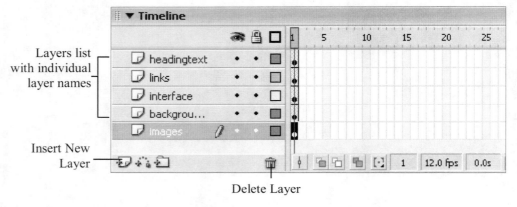

Exhibit 5-1: The Layers list in the Timeline panel

Creating layers

By default, layers are named in the order in which they are created. For example, the first layer is called Layer 1, the second layer is called Layer 2, and so on. However, when you delete layers, this automatic numbering does not re-count the existing layers and then produce the next number in that sequence. Therefore, if you create several layers and delete some of them, the default layer name will likely be a larger number than the actual number of layers in the document. You should always rename your layers anyway, because it's much easier to work with layers that have logical names that reflect the content they contain.

To create a layer, choose Insert, Layer, or click the New Layer button on the Timeline, as shown in Exhibit 5-1. A new layer appears above the currently active layer.

Do it!

A-1: Exploring layers

Here's how	**Here's why**
1 Open Layers.fla	(From the current unit folder.) This file contains shapes and images that are arranged in layers. In Flash, layers help you organize and modify shapes. You'll create a new layer in this document.
2 Save the file as **MyLayers**	In the current unit folder.
3 Display the Timeline panel	(If necessary.) Choose Window, Timeline.
4 Observe the Layers list	

The current file contains many layers, such as links, interface, background, and images.

Scroll through the Timeline panel	(Use the vertical scrollbar.) The images layer is the active layer. The active layer is indicated by a pencil symbol adjacent to the layer name.
Observe the Stage	Two images are selected, which indicates that these two images are on the same layer (the images layer). One of the images, the chef image, is currently half visible.
5 Activate the Selection tool	If necessary.
6 Click	

(The Insert Layer button is at the bottom of the Timeline panel.) You'll create a new layer and add an image to it.

7   Observe the Layers list

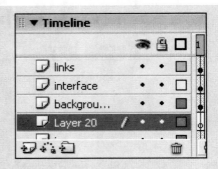

A new layer is added to the list. This layer has the default name Layer 20. The default name that Flash assigns to a layer will vary, and does not necessarily indicate the number of actual layers in a document.

8   Select the chili and onion image

9   Choose **Edit**, **Cut**

The image is removed from the images layer.

10 From the Layers list, select **Layer 20**

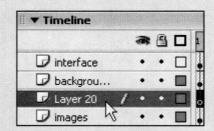

You'll add the image to this layer.

11 Choose **Edit**, **Paste in Place**

The garlic and chili image reappears on the Stage. Layer 20 is selected, which indicates that the image is part of this layer.

Deselect the image

12 Save your changes

Rearranging layers

Explanation

Layers are stacked like a stack of transparent papers. By default, the top-most layer in the Layers list appears at the top on the Stage. You can change the order of layers, which will affect the position of each layer and the objects on each layer. You can also merge any number of layers into a single layer.

Changing the stacking order of layers

To change the stacking order of a layer, drag the layer name to a new position in the list of layers. The list sequence represents the stacking order that appears on the Stage.

Merging layers

You can merge layers when you want the components of an image on separate layers to come together as a composite image. You can merge as many layers as you need. To merge layers:

1   Select the layers you want to merge. To select multiple layers, press and hold the Ctrl key and click the desired layers in the list.
2   Choose Edit, Cut. The selected layers are removed from the Stage.
3   Select the layer in which you want to place the content.
4   Choose Edit, Paste in Place. The content of the layers merge on the Stage.

Do it!

A-2:   Merging and rearranging layers

Here's how	Here's why
1 Verify that the Selection tool is activated	
2 From the Layers list, select **headingtext**	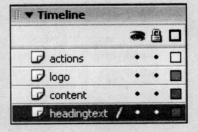
	You'll merge this layer with another layer.
3 Observe the Stage	
	There are two headings that are part of this layer, and they are both selected on the Stage.
4 Choose **Edit**, **Cut**	To remove these text headings.
5 From the Layers list, select **content**	You'll paste the heading text blocks in this layer.
6 Choose **Edit**, **Paste in Place**	To add the heading text blocks to the content layer.
7 Click the content layer	To select all the content in this layer. The contents of the two layers have been merged.
8 Observe the chef image	
	Only half of image appears because the background layer is above the images layer. To display the complete chef image, you'll need to shift the background layer below the images layer.

9   Select the **background** layer

10 Drag the **background** layer
    below the images layer as shown

As you drag the layer, a thatched line appears,
indicating the drop point.

11 Release the mouse button when
    the line is below the images layer

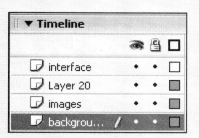

The background image is sent to the bottom of
the stacking order, which allows the chef image
to appear in full.

12 Observe the selection

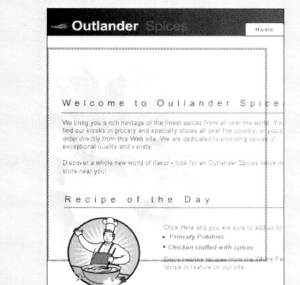

The boundary of the background layer shows
why the chef image was only half visible. The
background layer contains the plant image.

13 Save your changes

Deleting layers

Explanation

When you delete a layer, its content is removed from the Stage. To delete a layer, click the Delete Layer button or drag the layer to the Delete Layer button at the bottom of the Layers list. You can also right-click the layer and choose Delete Layer. It's important to delete unused layers because they needlessly increase the file size of your documents and make your layers more difficult to manage.

Do it!

A-3: Deleting a layer

Here's how	Here's why
1 Select the **headingtext** layer	You'll delete this layer.
2 Click 🗑	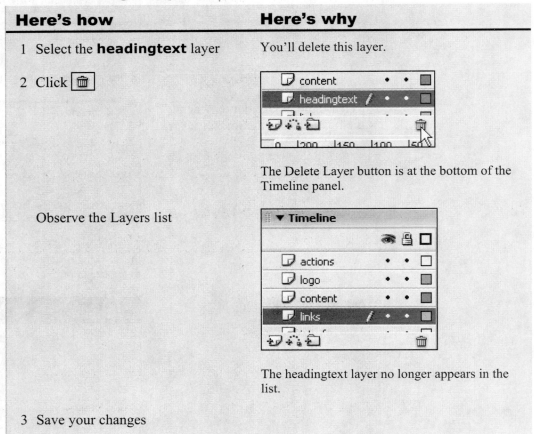 The Delete Layer button is at the bottom of the Timeline panel.
Observe the Layers list	The headingtext layer no longer appears in the list.
3 Save your changes	

Topic B: Modifying layers

Explanation

Flash gives every new layer a default name, but you can change these default names and make them more meaningful. A document with ten layers all named logically according to how they are used or the content they contain will be much easier to work with than a document with ten layers, all named Layer 1, Layer 2, etc. You should get in the habit of always giving your layers logical names. You can also prevent a layer from being modified. You can either lock a layer so it can't be edited, or hide it so that it's not visible.

Renaming layers

You rename layers in one of three ways:

- Choose Modify, Layer to open the Layer Properties dialog box. In the Name box, enter a new name.
- Right-click the layer and choose Properties to open the Layer Properties dialog box. Change the layer name and click OK.
- Double-click the layer, type a new name, and press Enter.

Do it!

B-1:   Renaming a layer

Here's how	Here's why
1 Right-click **Layer 20**	You'll rename this layer.
2 Choose **Properties...**	To open the Layer Properties dialog box.
3 Enter **spiceImage**	(In the Name box.) To specify a new name for the layer.
Click **OK**	The layer is renamed.
4 Observe the Timeline	
	The new layer name appears in the Layers list.
5 Rename the images layer **chefImage**	Right-click the images layer and choose Properties. Enter the new name and click OK.
6 Save your changes	

Locking layers

Explanation   Locking a layer helps prevent unwanted changes to that layer. When you lock a layer, a lock icon appears in the Lock column of the Layers list, as shown in Exhibit 5-2. When you lock a layer, you can't use any tools to modify that layer. This prevents any inadvertent changes to a layer.

To lock a layer, you can:

- Next to the layer name in the Layers list, click the dot in the Lock column.
- Open the Layer Properties dialog box and check the Lock option for that layer.

To unlock a layer, you can:

- Next to the layer name in the Layers list, click the lock icon in the Lock column.
- Open the Layer Properties dialog box and clear the Lock option for that layer.

To lock all layers except the selected layer, right-click the selected layer and choose Lock Others. To lock or unlock all layers, click the Lock/Unlock All Layers button (the lock icon), shown in Exhibit 5-2.

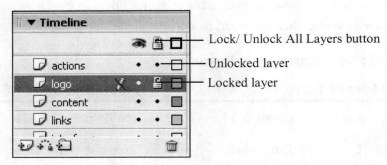

Exhibit 5-2: Locked and unlocked layers

Hiding layers

If you need to modify a layer that's below another layer, you can hide the top layer. When you hide a layer, its content disappears from the Stage. You can't edit or print the content of a hidden layer. To hide a layer, you click the dot in the Eye column or open the Layer Properties dialog box and clear Show option for that layer.

A red "X" appears in the Eye column for a hidden layer, as shown in Exhibit 5-3, and the content of that layer disappears from the Stage.

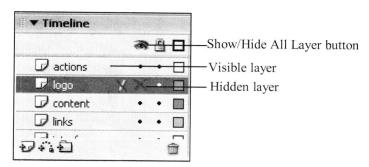

Exhibit 5-3: Hidden and visible layers

To show a hidden layer, you click the red X in the Eye column or open the Layer Properties dialog box and check the Show option for that layer.

To hide all layers except the selected layer, right-click the selected layer and choose Hide Others. To unlock these layers, right-click the selected layer and choose Show All. To hide all layers in a document, click the Show/Hide All Layers button (the eye icon).

Do it!

B-2: Locking and hiding layers

Here's how	Here's why
1 Verify that the **chefImage** layer is selected	(In the Layers list.) You'll lock this layer.
2 Click the dot in the Lock column	To lock the layer.
Observe the layer	
	A lock appears in the Lock column, and the pencil icon has a red line through it. This indicates that you cannot modify the shapes or images on this layer.
3 Activate the Oval tool	You'll try to edit the locked layer.
Try to draw an oval on the Stage	A message appears warning you that the layer is either locked or hidden.
Click **No**	
4 Click the dot in the Eye column	
	To hide this layer from the Stage. The dot changes to a red X, which indicates that the layer is hidden.
5 Observe the Stage	The chef image no longer appears on it.
6 Click the red X	
	To show the layer. The chef image reappears.

7 Right-click the **chefImage** layer   You'll hide all layers but this one.

   Choose **Hide Others**

To hide all layers except the chefImage layer. A red X appears in the Eye column of all other layers.

8 Right-click the **chefImage** layer   You'll show all the layers.

   Choose **Show All**   All layers are again visible on the Stage.

9 Save your changes

Adding a mask layer

Explanation

Mask layers provide a simple way to show select portions of a layer or layers below it. To mask a layer, one layer is designated as a mask layer and the layers below it are designated as masked layers. The shapes on a mask layer hide the rest of the shapes on the Stage and reveal only the shapes that are not under the mask.

To mask a layer:

1 Add a layer above the layer that contains the image you want to mask.

2 Create a shape on the new layer.

3 Drag the shape onto the image you want to mask.

4 In the Timeline, right-click the layer containing the shape and choose Mask from the list. The layer converts to a mask layer, and the layer immediately below is the masked layer. The masked layer's name is indented under the layer.

Do it!

B-3: Masking a layer

Here's how	Here's why
1 Create a new layer above the spiceImage layer	
	(Right-click the spiceImage layer and choose Insert Layer.) You'll mask the spiceImage layer.
2 Rename the new layer **ovalMask**	Double-click the layer name, type ovalMask, and press Enter.
3 Activate the Oval tool	If necessary.
Draw a circle on the spice image, as shown	

4 Right-click the ovalMask layer

Choose **Mask**

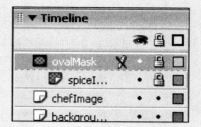

To convert the layer to a mask layer. The
spiceImage layer is indented under the
ovalMask layer. The mask layer and the layer it
masks are automatically locked.

Observe the image

Only the part of the image that was inside by the
circle is visible. The rest of the image is masked.

5 Save your changes

Layer folders

Explanation

You can organize layers in folders to group related layers and keep your documents well organized. To create folders:

1 At the bottom of the Timeline panel, click the Insert Layer Folder button. A new folder is added above the selected layer.

2 Rename the new folder.

3 Drag the layers to the folder. The layers appear indented towards right to indicate that they're within the folder. You can then click the expander arrow to collapse or expand the folder.

Do it!

B-4: Creating layer folders

Here's how	Here's why
1 From the Layers list, select **chefImage**	
2 Click 🗂	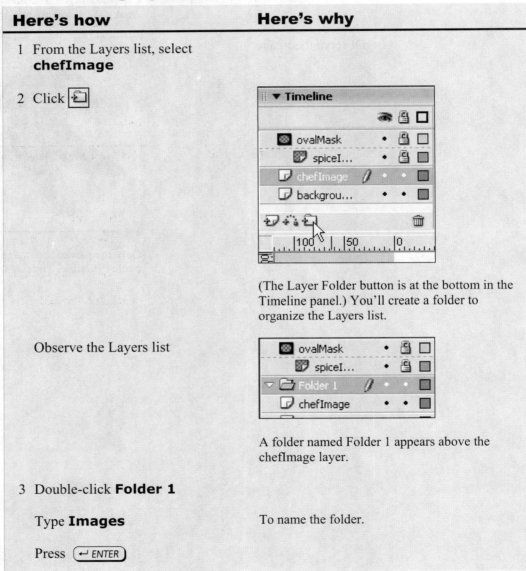 (The Layer Folder button is at the bottom in the Timeline panel.) You'll create a folder to organize the Layers list.
Observe the Layers list	A folder named Folder 1 appears above the chefImage layer.
3 Double-click **Folder 1**	
Type **Images**	To name the folder.
Press ◄┘ ENTER	

4 Drag the **chefImage** layer to
   the Images folder, as shown

The chefImage layer is indented under the
folder, indicating that it's inside the folder.

5 Drag the **background** layer to
   the Images folder

Under the chefImage layer.

   Drag the **ovalMask** layer to the
   top of the Images folder

The three layers are indented under the Images
folder.

6 Click the expander arrow as
   indicated

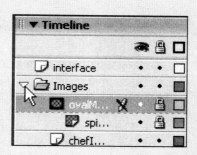

To collapse the folder and the layers inside it.

7 Save your changes

Topic C: Guide layers

Explanation

You use *guide layers* to hold content that you don't want to show in a published file. For example, you can place rectangles or lines on a layer that will serve as guides for specifying the position of other images. You can even write notes to other developers who might need to edit a document, or enter text in a document that provides information such as the author, last published date, or any other information about the file that might be helpful to you or other developers.

Creating a guide layer

To create a guide layer:

1   Select a layer or create a new layer to designate as a guide layer.

2   Right-click the layer and choose Guide. A guide icon appears next to the layer name.

3   On the guide layer, create any shapes or lines that can be used as a guide for precisely positioning objects.

4   Choose Control, Test Movie to export the Flash file to a shockwave file. Objects on a guide layer do not appear in the published file.

Publishing a Flash document for testing

The Flash files you work in (.fla files) are not the same files that users will view on the Web. When you're done creating a Flash movie, you should publish it to test how it will appear in a browser. To test a Flash movie, choose Control, Test Movie (or press Ctrl+Enter), Flash exports the document to a shockwave file, which is a completed, "published" version of the Flash document. Shockwave files have a .swf file extension, and can be viewed in Web browsers, while Flash documents (.fla files) cannot. When you publish a Flash document, the shockwave file is saved to the same folder as the Flash file.

Do it!

C-1: Creating a guide layer

Here's how	Here's why
1 Insert a new layer above the content layer	You'll designate this layer as a guide layer to hold content that will not appear in the published file.
2 Name the new layer **Notes**	
3 Right-click the **Notes** layer	
Choose **Guide**	
Observe the Layers list	

A guide icon appears on the Notes layer.

4 Draw a text box and type **Last Edited by (your name)**	

The text in a guide layer will be of use to you and other developers, but will not appear in the published file.

Deselect the text block

5 Save your changes

6 Choose **Control**, **Test Movie** — A message appears indicating that Flash is exporting the document. When it's done, the published shockwave document is displayed. This is how the document will appear to the end user. The content in the guide layer is not visible.

7 Close the MyLayers.swf window — To close the published shockwave file.

8 Close the MyLayers.fla window

Unit summary: Layers

Topic A   In this topic, you learned how to work with **layers**. You learned that layers are like transparent pieces of paper stacked on top of each other, which allow you to edit specific images and shapes without affecting other areas. You also learned how to create a new layer, **rearrange** and **merge** layers, and delete a layer.

Topic B   In this topic, you learned how to modify layers. You learned how to name a layer, and how to **lock** layers to prevent them from being modified. You also learned how to **hide** a layer, and how to **mask** a layer to display only specific portions of a layer or the layers below that layer. You also learned how to organize layers by creating folders.

Topic C   In this topic, you learned how to create a **guide layer**. You learned that you can use guide layers to hold information for you or other developers, such as the author name or last modified date, instructions, warnings, or other valuable information that is not meant to be displayed in the published file.

Independent practice activity

1 Open Layers practice.fla.

2 Save the file as **My Layers practice** in the current unit folder.

3 Create a new layer and name it **Text**.

4 Move all the text blocks into the **Text** layer.

5 Add another layer and rename it as **images**.

6 Lock the **images** layer.

7 Create a guide layer named **Developer Notes**. In this layer, create a text block and enter **Last modified by (your name)**, followed by today's date.

8 Save and close the file. Don't close Flash.

Unit 6

Animation

Unit time: 100 minutes

Complete this unit, and you'll know how to:

A Create a basic text animation.

B Create a frame-by-frame animation, use the Library, create graphic symbols, modify symbol instances, and use Onion Skin to modify an animation.

C Create a shape tweened animation and a motion tweened animation, use shape hints and motion guides, and arrange and extend frames on the Timeline.

Topic A: *Animation basics*

Explanation

In Flash, you can create "movies," which are animations of vector drawings, images, sound, video, and other content. So far, you've explored the basics of using the Flash tools, and you have drawn objects, changed colors, created layers, and applied text to the Stage. All of these skills are required to create and modify an animation. In this unit, you will learn the basics of creating animations in Flash.

An *animation* is a series of related shapes and images that create an illusion of motion when they are shown in a sequence. You can create an animation by creating shapes or text that move or appear on the Stage, or by making shapes or text change parameters like color or size.

Playing an animation

At any time during the development of a Flash movie, you can test its progress by choosing Control, Play or by pressing the Enter key. This gives you an opportunity to check your work in progress and make any required changes. The movie will play in the Flash window just as it would as a finished product in a user's browser.

Do it!

A-1:   Exploring an animation

Here's how	Here's why
1 Open Animation demo.fla	(From the current unit folder.) This is an animation demonstration that can serve as an intro for the Outlander Spices Web site.
From the Zoom box, select **Show All**	
2 Press (↵ ENTER)	To play the animation directly in the Flash workspace. The red color fills move to the center, followed by a chili image, which changes to a rectangle, then a circle, and finally disappears. Text then moves from the top to the center. This is a simple example of the kind of animations you can create with Flash.
3 Close the file	

The Timeline

Explanation

To create Flash movies, you need to learn about the Timeline and frames. The *Timeline* panel allows you to control the behavior of an animation. An animation consists of frames. A frame is a point in time along the Timeline—a placeholder in which you insert images or shapes that will appear at a given point in time. Each layer in a movie has its own frames.

The Timeline is divided into two sections, shown in Exhibit 6-1. The area on the left contains the layers in the document, and the area on the right contains the Timeline, the frames, and the *playhead*, which is an indicator that marks the progression of a movie or animation over time.

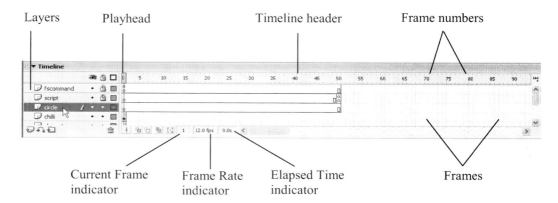

Exhibit 6-1: The Timeline

The following table describes the various components of the Timeline:

Item	Description
Playhead	Marks the progression of a movie or animation over time. As the playhead moves, the contents in the frame below it appear on the Stage.
Current Frame indicator	Displays the frame number corresponding to the position of the playhead.
Frame Rate indicator	Displays the number of frames over which the playhead moves in one second. By default, the playhead moves over the Timeline covering 12 frames per second. You can change the Frame Rate by double-clicking the Frame Rate box. The Document Properties dialog box opens, where you can specify a new Frame Rate value.
Elapsed Time indicator	Displays the time that the playhead takes to move over all the frames in the animation. The value in the Elapsed Time box is related to the value in the Frame Rate box. The higher the frame rate, the shorter the elapsed time, and vice versa.

The status bar on the Timeline shows the current frame number, the frame rate, and the elapsed time, as shown at the bottom of Exhibit 6-1.

Do it!

A-2: Exploring the timeline

Here's how	Here's why
1 Open Basic animation.fla	(From the current unit folder.) You'll explore the Timeline for this file.
From the Zoom list, select **Show All**	
2 Save the file as **My Basic animation**	In the current unit folder.
3 Hide all panels	(If necessary.) Except the Timeline.
4 Observe the Timeline header	
	The numbers in the Timeline header indicate the frame numbers.
5 In the Timeline, point as shown	
	This is the Current Frame indicator. It displays the frame number that corresponds to the position of the playhead.
Point as shown	
	This is the Frame Rate indicator. It displays the number of frames played per second. The default rate is 12 frames per second, but you can change this value.
Point as shown	
	This is the Elapsed Time indicator. It displays the time that the playhead takes to move over all the frames in the animation.

Frames and keyframes

While a frame represents a point in time along the Timeline, a *keyframe* is a frame in which a change to the animation is defined. Keyframes that contain content are indicated on the Timeline by a black circle on the frame and a gray background. A blank keyframe is a keyframe that does not contain any content, and is indicated by a hollow circle on the frame and a white background, as shown in Exhibit 6-2. An empty rectangle indicates the end of a keyframe segment.

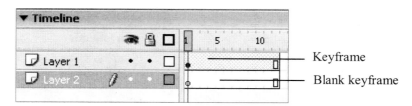

Exhibit 6-2: A keyframe and a blank keyframe

It's easy to manipulate keyframes on the Timeline. You can drag keyframes to different locations along the Timeline. You can also insert them anywhere along the Timeline by choosing Insert, Timeline, Keyframe, or by right-clicking a frame and choosing Insert Keyframe.

Animating text

One way to create a basic text animation is to break apart the characters in a line of text and distribute them to individual layers. By placing each character on its own layer, you can control the behavior of each layer individually. To break text into individual characters:

1 Select the text box.

2 Choose Modify, Break Apart.

3 Choose Modify, Timeline, Distribute to Layers.

Each character will have its own layer, automatically named according to each layer. You can then use the Timeline to apply changes to the separate layers to create an animation effect.

For example, you can use the Timeline to make each layer appear at a different moment in time, which would create the illusion of the text being typed on the screen.

Do it!

A-3: Creating a basic text animation

Here's how	Here's why
1 Observe the Text layer on the Timeline	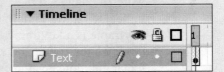
	The keyframe contains a black circle, which indicates that there is content on the Stage at this point in time.
2 Activate the Selection tool	
Select the text	You'll animate this text.
3 Choose **Modify, Break Apart**	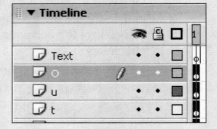
	To set each character in the text as a separate shape.
4 Choose **Modify, Timeline, Distribute To Layers**	To distribute each character of text to its own layer.
Observe the Timeline	
	(Scroll through the Timeline to view all the layers.) Each character is distributed to an individual layer. Also note that the Text layer has an empty circle in its frame, indicating that the layer no longer contains content. This is a blank keyframe.
5 Right-click the Text layer and choose **Delete Layer**	To delete the Text layer. This layer no longer has content because you distributed the text to individual layers.
Observe the Stage	The text is not deleted because each character resides in its own layer.

6 Expand the Timeline vertically

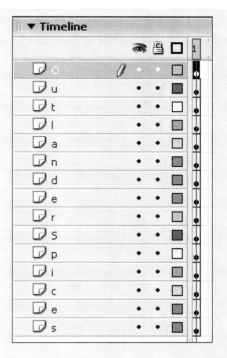

To view all the layers.

7 On the O layer, select frame **20**

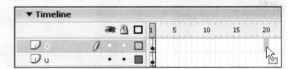

Press and hold SHIFT

You will select multiple frames.

On the last layer, select frame **20**

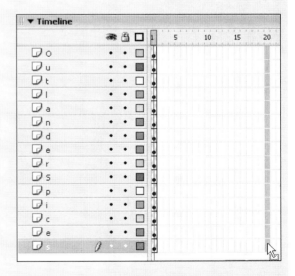

To select frame 20 for all the layers.

Release SHIFT

8 Choose **Insert**, **Timeline**, **Frame**

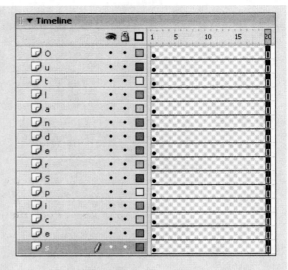

To add frames to all of the layers. Note that Flash fills in the entire region with a gray color.

Observe the Timeline status bar

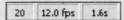

The status bar indicates that there are now 20 frames, and at the default frame rate of 12 frames per second, this animation will take 1.6 seconds to complete.

9 On the first layer, drag the keyframe to the third frame, as shown

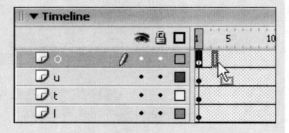

The O will not appear on the Stage until the playhead reaches the third frame.

10 On the second layer, drag the keyframe to the fifth frame

The u will not appear on the Stage until the playhead reaches the fifth frame.

11 On the third layer, drag the
    keyframe to the seventh frame

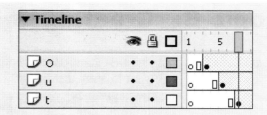

The t will not appear on the Stage until the
playhead reaches the seventh frame.

12 Move the keyframes for the
    remaining layers so that they
    increase by one frame, as shown

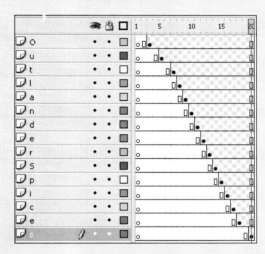

Each layer begins with a blank keyframe, which
means that none of the layers will display when
the animation starts. When the playhead reaches
the keyframe for each layer, that layer's content
will be displayed on the Stage.

13 On the Timeline header, click **1**

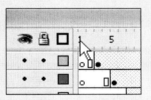

To bring the playhead back to the beginning.
Note that no text appears on the Stage at the
starting point of the animation.

14 Press (↵ ENTER)

To start the playhead and view the animation.
Each character appears in sequence, according
to the settings on the Timeline. This creates the
appearance of the text being typed on screen.

15 Save your changes and close the
    file

Topic B: Creating and manipulating animations

Explanation

The first step in the creation of a frame-by-frame animation is to create the image you want to animate. To build the animation, you add the modified versions of the image to the keyframes you insert in the Timeline. You can view the components of all the keyframes and then modify them separately.

Animation types

There are two animation types in Flash, frame-by-frame and tweened animations. When you create a *frame-by-frame* animation, you need to manually create each different variation of the shapes in the sequence. It's similar to the original way in which animations were created, that is, using a flipbook where each consecutive page contains an image that moves slightly. When the pages are turned or "flipped" quickly, the small sequential changes create the illusion of motion. In a frame-by-frame animation, all frames are keyframes.

In *tweened* animation, you need to simply create shapes for the start and end of the animation. Flash automatically creates the intermediate content, or the content in be*tween* the start and end shapes.

To create a frame-by-frame animation:

1   Create an image. By default, this image is automatically placed in the keyframe on the Timeline.

2   In the Timeline, click the frame where you want to insert the keyframe.

3   Choose Insert, Keyframe to insert the keyframe. You can also press F6 or right-click and select Insert Keyframe.

4   Modify the image in the keyframe.

5   Repeat steps 2 through 4 to add more keyframes.

Storing layers off the Stage

One way to work with layers and create animations is to store your layers off the Stage until they're needed in the animation. This is particularly useful if you want to create the illusion of content moving onto the Stage. When you keep layers in the work area off the Stage, you will likely need to zoom out on the Stage to view all the content in the work area.

Working with symbols and the library

A *symbol* is an object that can be reused in a Flash document. Symbols can be graphics, buttons, video clips, sound files, or fonts. They reduce the file size of a Flash movie because only one copy of the image or shape is stored, yet you can use it as many times as necessary. You should use symbols whenever you have an object that appears more than once in a document.

To convert an existing shape, bitmap, or image on the Stage into a symbol, select the shape and choose Modify, Convert to Symbol (or press F8). This opens the Convert to Symbol dialog box, shown in Exhibit 6-3. In the Name box, give your symbol a meaningful name, just as you would give a layer a meaningful name. By default, Flash will create a graphic symbol. Click OK to convert the image or shape to a graphic symbol, which you can reuse multiple times without increasing the movie's file size.

Convert to Symbol

Name: Symbol 1

Behavior: ⦿ Movie clip   Registration: ▪☐☐   OK
       ○ Button   ☐☐☐   Cancel
       ○ Graphic   ☐☐☐   Advanced

Exhibit 6-3: The Convert to Symbol dialog box

When you create a symbol, it is stored in the library, which you view by choosing
Window, Library to open the Library panel. The Library panel lists all the symbols in
your Flash document, as well as any imported files. Every item in the library has an icon
that identifies its file type. When you click a symbol in the Library, a preview of that
symbol appears in the preview pane, as shown in Exhibit 6-4. You can re-use a symbol
as many times as necessary by dragging it from the Library to the Stage. When you do
so, you create an *instance* of that symbol—an occurrence of that symbol on the Stage.

Exhibit 6-4: The Library panel, containing one graphic symbol

B-1: Creating a basic frame-by-frame animation

Here's how	Here's why
1 Open Animation1.fla	This Flash document contains one layer, an image of chili peppers.
From the Zoom list, choose **100%**	(If necessary.) To view the Stage and the work area. Note that the layer is currently off the Stage. You'll create an animation of the chili peppers moving across the Stage.
2 Save the file as **MyAnimation1**	
3 Select the image	
4 Choose **Modify**, **Convert to Symbol...**	To open the Convert to Symbol dialog box, as shown in Exhibit 6-3. You'll convert this image to a graphic symbol, which you can reuse multiple times.
In the Name box, enter **chilies**	
	To give the symbol a name.
Select **Graphic**	If necessary.
Click **OK**	To convert the image to a graphic symbol.
5 Choose **Window**, **Library**	To open the Library panel. Your graphic symbol appears in the library.
Click the chilies icon	A preview of the symbol appears, as shown in Exhibit 6-4. Now that you have converted this image to a symbol, you're ready to animate it.
6 Close the Library panel	

7 Right-click frame 3 for the chilies layer and choose **Insert Keyframe**

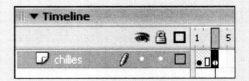

A keyframe is inserted on frame 3.

8 Drag the image to the center left edge of the Stage, as shown

9 Insert a keyframe in frame 5

   Move the image slightly to the right

10 Insert a keyframe in frame 7

    Move the image further to the right

11 Insert a keyframe in frame 9

    Move the image further to the right

12 Press (↵ ENTER)

    To play the movie. The image of the chili moves from the left toward the center of the Stage.

13 Save your changes and close the file

Editing symbols

Explanation

You can make changes to an instance, and it will not affect the "master" symbol that's stored in the library. You can also edit the master symbol if you want to change all instances of that symbol in the document. You edit symbols in three modes: Edit, Edit In Place, and Edit In New Window. To edit a symbol:

- Right-click the symbol and choose Edit In Place. This mode allows you to edit only the selected symbol without affecting other symbols. All other symbols appear dimmed.
- Right-click the symbol and choose Edit In New Window. This opens the symbol in a new document window with a new Timeline for that symbol.
- Double-click the symbol icon in the Library to open the symbol in Edit mode. (You can also right-click and choose Edit to open the symbol in Edit mode.)

Modifying graphic symbols

You can modify a graphic symbol in the same way that you modify a regular graphic on the Stage. You can rotate or scale it, change its fill and stroke colors, or transform it. You can also use its transformation point, the small circle that appears in the center of the symbol when you select the Transformation tool. You can position and set the behavior of a shape relative to its transformation point.

Using Onion Skin

When viewing an animation in a non-playing state, only the content of the selected frame appears on the Stage. By default, the content of the first frame appears. It's often helpful to view the content of all your keyframes when you're creating an animation. You can do this by using *Onion Skin*. When you use Onion Skin, the content for each keyframe appears slightly dimmed on the Stage. To use Onion Skin, click the Onion Skin button at the bottom of the Timeline, as shown in Exhibit 6-5. Onion Skin markers appear on the Timeline. You drag these markers to display the content of all the keyframes. You can then modify all the keyframes at the same time by using the Edit Multiple Frames button at the bottom of the Timeline.

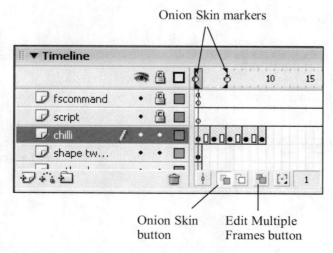

Exhibit 6-5: A part of the Timeline

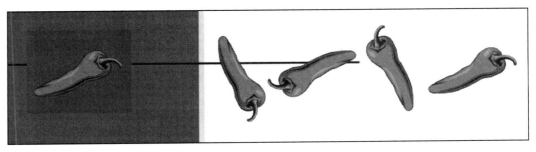

Exhibit 6-6: Rotated instances of the graphic symbol

Do it!

B-2:   Using Onion Skin to modify an animation

Here's how	Here's why
1 Open Animation2.fla	This document contains several existing graphic symbols. You will use Onion Skin to create a frame-by-frame animation.
From the Zoom list, select **Show All**	This document contains several existing layers, all currently off the Stage, except for a portion of the black line. The animation on the chili layer is just like the animation you created earlier.
2 Save the file as **MyAnimation2**	
3 Verify that the chili layer is selected	You'll modify the keyframes on the chili layer to create the effect of a rotating chili.
Select frame 1	On the Timeline.
4 Click	(The Onion Skin button is at the bottom of the Timeline.) The position of the symbol for the first frame is displayed, and is slightly dimmed.
Observe the Timeline	Onion Skin markers appear on the Timeline scale. The left marker over frame 1 indicates the starting frame for the Onion Skin effect, and the right marker indicates the frame where the Onion Skin effect ends.

5 Drag the right Onion Skin marker to frame 9, as shown

Observe the Stage

The position of the image in each keyframe is displayed. The position of each image will create the illusion of motion across the Stage. Using Onion Skin can make it easier to create precise edits between keyframes.

6 Click

(The Edit Multiple Frames button is at the bottom of the Timeline.) You'll modify the contents of multiple frames at the same time. Note that the images no longer appear dimmed on the Stage.

7 Select the third chili on the Stage

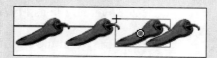

(Use the Selection tool.) You will move this image to make all four chilies more evenly spaced.

Drag the chili slightly to the left, as shown

The chilies are now more evenly spaced.

8 Select the first chili on the Stage

Choose **Modify**, **Transform**, **Rotate 90° CW**

To rotate the chili by 90 degrees.

9 Select the second chili on the
   Stage

   Choose **Modify**, **Transform**,
   Rotate 90° CW

   Again, choose **Modify**,
   Transform, **Rotate 90° CW**

   To rotate the image 180° clockwise.

10 Select the third chili on the Stage

   Choose **Modify**, **Transform**,
   Rotate 90° CCW

   To rotate the image 90° counter-clockwise (or
   the equivalent of 270° clockwise).

11 Click 🔳   (The Edit Multiple Frames button.) To deselect
                                 the image in each keyframe.

   Click 🔳   (The Onion Skin button.) To hide the contents of
                                 the keyframes.

12 Drag the playhead to the second
   frame

   Play the document   (Press Enter.) The chili appears to tumble in
                                 toward the center of the Stage.

13 Save your changes

Topic C: Tweening and hinting

Explanation

You can create an animation by tweening images and shapes. Tweening is a technique that fills the frames between two frames to create an animation. Tweened animation is an effective way to create the illusion of movement while keeping the file size to a minimum because Flash only needs to store information about the starting and ending keyframes, not the tweened frames. You can tween objects in two ways, motion and shape. *Motion tweening* creates an animation with a moving effect and *shape tweening* morphs one shape into another.

Shape tweening and hinting

With shape tweening, you can make one shape appear to morph into another shape over a set period of time. Flash can tween any properties, including the location, size, and color, of shapes. You cannot shape tween groups or text blocks, but you can break them apart to convert them into shapes, and then shape tween them. To break apart shapes, text blocks, or groups, select the text block or the group that you want to break apart, and choose Modify, Break Apart.

To create a shape tween:

1   Select the layer and create a keyframe where you want the animation to start.
2   Place the shape for the first frame.
3   Select the keyframe on the Timeline.
4   In the Properties panel, from the Tween list, select Shape.
5   Create a second keyframe and select the shape from the first frame while keeping the second keyframe selected.
6   Delete the shape in the second keyframe and paste the new shape into it.

Hinting

Flash sometimes needs hints to create the morph you're looking for. The starting an ending shapes are always the same, but the default tween shapes that Flash creates might not look the way you want them to. To control the tweening effect, use Shape hints to mark points that correspond to the starting and ending shapes. Shape hints are markers that help Flash create more specific shape tweens.

When you add a Shape hint to a starting shape, a corresponding hint is added to the ending shape. If you add three hints to a starting shape, three hints are automatically added to its ending shape. Shape hints are labeled a to z to make it easy to view corresponding points. For example, Shape hint "a" on the starting shape corresponds to Shape hint "a" on the ending shape. The color of a Shape hint varies according to its keyframe. Shape hints turn yellow in a starting keyframe and green in an ending keyframe. When shape hints remain red, the hints are not matched up—typically because one or more hints are not on a line or curve. A circle with two shape hints is shown in Exhibit 6-7.

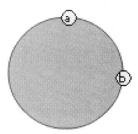

Exhibit 6-7: Shape hints, labeled a and b.

To use shape hints:

1   Create a keyframe on a selected frame.
2   Select Modify, Shape, Add Shape Hint.
3   Place the first shape hint on the starting shape.
4   Create the second shape hint and place it on the ending shape.
5   Move to another frame and adjust the shape hints accordingly.

C-1: Using shape tweening and hinting

Here's how	Here's why
1 Drag the playhead to frame 1	If necessary.
Select the **shape tween** layer	The image of a chili and a square is visible on the left side of the Stage. The square is selected.
2 Choose **Edit**, **Cut**	To cut the shape.
Insert a keyframe in frame 9	

(For the shape tween layer.) The shape will appear in the animation starting in frame 9.

From the Zoom list, select **Show Frame**	
3 Choose **Edit**, **Paste in Center**	To paste the shape in the center of the Stage.
Select the chili layer	
Drag the chili so that it appears in the middle of the square	

Select the **shape tween** layer	
4 Insert a blank keyframe on frame 15	

For the shape tween layer.

5 Draw a circle	(Any size and location will do.) The square will change into this circle when the animation reaches frame 15.
Delete the stroke of the circle	Select the outer edge of the circle with the Selection tool, and press Delete.
Select the circle	Click it.

6 Display the Property inspector	If necessary.
Expand the Property inspector	If necessary.
7 Change the values of W, H, X and Y as shown	
	(In the Property inspector.) To change the height, width, and position of the circle on the Stage.
Change the fill color of the circle to **990000**	If necessary.
8 Select frame 10	(On the shape tween layer.) You'll create a shape tween for the rectangle.
From the Tween list, select **Shape**, as shown	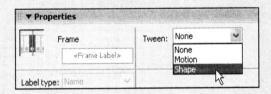
	(In the Property inspector.) To shape tween the rectangle.
9 Observe the Timeline	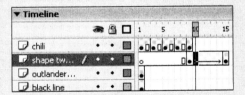
	The tween is indicated by a light green color in the frames between the two shapes, and an arrow from the starting keyframe to the ending keyframe.
Play the document	(Press Enter.) The square gradually changes to a circle.
10 Drag the playhead to frame 9	
Copy the rectangle	(Select it and choose Edit, Copy.) You'll make the circle turn back into the rectangle.

11 Insert a keyframe on frame 25   For the shape tween layer.

    Delete the circle

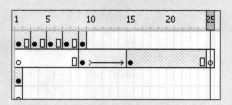

(Press Delete.) Frame 25 now shows a blank keyframe.

12 Choose **Edit**, **Paste in Place**   To paste the rectangle in the same location from which it was copied. The keyframe no longer appears as a blank keyframe.

13 Select any frame between 15 and 25

    From the Tween list, select **Shape**   To create a new shape tween.

    Move the playhead between frames 15 and 25

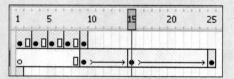

To observe how the shape morphs. The square morphs into a circle and then back into a square. Now you'll add a shape hint to the circle on frame 15.

14 Select frame 15

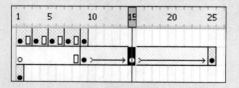

For the shape tween layer.

    Deselect the shape on the Stage   Click any white area on the Stage.

15 Choose **View,**
    Show Shape Hints

To select the Show Shape Hints option.

Choose **Modify**, **Shape**,
Add Shape Hint

To add a shape hint to the rectangle.

Observe the Stage

A red shape hint appears in the middle of the
circle with the label a.

16 Drag the shape hint to the
    "two o'clock" position

Add another shape hint and drag it
to the "five o'clock" position

(Choose Modify, Shape, Add Shape Hint.)
Notice that the shape hint has the label b.

17 Select the keyframe on frame 25

Observe the Stage

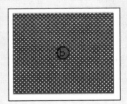

In the center of the rectangle, there are two
shape hints, labeled a and b. The shape hint
labeled b currently overlaps shape hint a.

18 Move the shape hints to the
    indicated positions

    Click any white area of the Stage

To deselect the shape. The shape hints for the
end shape are green. This indicates that they are
matched up successfully.

19 Select frame 15

The shape hints for the starting shape are now
yellow, which indicates the starting shape hints
are matched up with their corresponding end
points.

20 Move the playhead from frame 15
    and 25, and back

Notice how the shape hints affect the tweened
shapes.

21 Select the keyframe on frame 25

You'll change the shape hints on the rectangle.

    Move the shape hint labeled a to
    the indicated position

    Move the playhead from frame 15
    and 25, and back

The new placement of the shape hints change
the way the shapes appear to transform.

22 Choose **View**,
    Show Shape Hints

To turn off the shape hints. The changes remain,
but the shape hint labels are not displayed.

    Save your changes

Motion tweening

Explanation

Motion tweening creates the illusion of motion between shapes. For example, instead of manually changing the position of a bird in different frames, you can specify the starting and ending keyframes and let Flash create the motion between the frames. Motion tweening moves an image or shape one step closer to its end point in each successive frame. It happens in a straight line between two points.

You can also define properties such as position, size, and rotation, for an instance, group, or text block, and change these properties as needed.

To create a motion tween:

1 Select the object on the first frame.
2 Create a keyframe where you want the tweening effect to end.
3 Move the object to the desired position.
4 Select any keyframe between the first and last keyframes.
5 In the Property inspector, from the Tween list, choose Motion.

You can also right-click a frame and choose Create Motion Tween.

Moving objects on the Stage

Dragging objects is a fast and easy way to move objects around the Stage. However, if you want to be more precise, you can use the arrow keys on your keyboard. Pressing any of the four arrow keys will move the image or shape slightly in that direction. You can also press Shift+arrow key to move an object more quickly on the Stage. This creates a "Tab key" effect, where the object will move at intervals.

Do it!

C-2: Using motion tweening

Here's how	Here's why
1 Drag the playhead to frame 1	
2 Select the left red box layer	To select the red rectangle on the left side of the Stage.
3 Insert a keyframe in frame 5	
Observe the Stage	The chili appears in this frame of the animation.
4 From the Zoom list, select **Show All**	
5 Move the left red box fully onto the Stage	
	Make the left edge of the red box flush with the left edge of the Stage.
Move the playhead back to **1**	
6 Select the right red box layer	

7 Insert a keyframe in frame 5

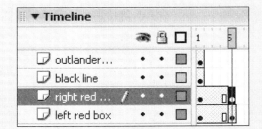

8 Drag the right red box so that it fills the remaining area on the Stage

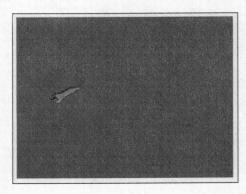

To give the entire Stage a red background.

9 Select any frame between 1 and 5, as shown

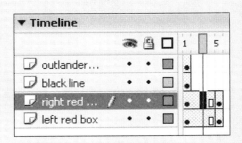

For the right red box layer.

From the Tween list, select **Motion**

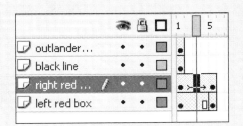

(In the Property inspector.) Notice that the area in between the keyframes is now a pale blue color with an arrow. This indicates a motion tween.

Right-click frame 3 of the left red box layer and choose **Create Motion Tween**

10 Drag the playhead to frame 1	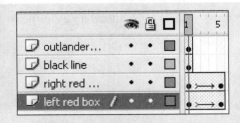
Drag the playhead to frame 5	The red boxes appear to move to the center of the Stage.
11 Drag the playhead to frame 1	
Select the **black line** layer	You'll create motion tween for the black line.
12 Insert a keyframe in frame 5	
Press and hold (SHIFT)	
Press the right arrow key several times until it reaches the indicated position	
	Make the left edge of the black line flush against the left edge of the Stage.
Release (SHIFT)	
13 Insert a keyframe in frame 10	For the black line layer.
Select the line on the Stage	(Click it.) You'll modify its properties.
Change the line's height to **80**	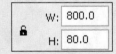
	(On the Property inspector.) To increase the height of the black line.

14 Press (⏎ ENTER)   To apply the new height value.

Move the black line so that it lines up behind the shape, as shown

15 Create a motion tween between frames 1 and 5

Create a motion tween between frames 5 and 10

16 Drag the playhead between frames 1 and 10   To observe the motion tweens. The black line appears to move into the center of the Stage, and then increase in size.

17 Save your changes

Tweening with a guide

Explanation   Motion tweening moves an image or shape in a straight line, but you can also make a motion tween follow a curved path. You can define a path, called a *guide line,* in a separate layer called a guide layer. To associate shapes with the guide, you need to attach the shapes in the first and last frames to the end points of the guide line.

You can also link multiple layers to a motion guide layer so that multiple objects follow the same path. Any layer linked to a motion guide layer functions as a guided layer.

To create a motion tween by using a guide:

1   Select the layer on which you want to apply the motion tween.
2   Right-click and choose Add Motion Guide, or click the Add Motion Guide button on the Timeline.
3   On the Guide layer, draw a path for the motion by using the Pen or Pencil tool.
4   Create the motion tween.

When you have successfully created a guide layer and have tested it, you can hide it by clicking the dot in the Eye column of the guide layer. This will make the guide path invisible for the finished product. However, don't delete your guide layers, or your motion tween will not have a path to follow, and will move in a straight line instead.

Do it!

C-3: Using motion tweening with a guide

Here's how	Here's why
1 Drag the playhead to frame 1	
Select the **outlander text** layer	You'll animate this text moving onto the Stage.
2 Right-click the layer and choose **Add Motion Guide**	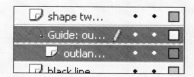
	A new layer is added above the outlander text layer with the prefix Guide. Both layers are selected. By default, the guide layer extends to the current longest frame.
Insert a blank keyframe in frame 10	Of the guide layer.
3 Select the first frame of the outlander text layer	
Drag the keyframe to frame 10	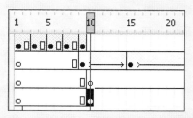
	This is the point in the Timeline where the text will first appear.
4 Hide the shape tween layer	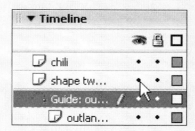
	(Click the dot in the Eye column of the shape tween layer.) To temporarily hide this layer so that you can work more easily in this keyframe.
5 Select the **Guide** layer	

6   Activate the Pencil tool

On the Toolbar, select **Smooth**

You'll draw a guide path.

(In the Options section.) To make sure the motion follows a smooth line.

7   Draw a curved line as shown

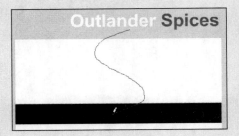

The motion tween will follow this path.

Activate the Selection tool

8   Select **Outlander Spices**

Using the center point, drag the text so that the circle snaps to the starting point of the guide path

9   Select the **outlander text** layer

10 Insert a keyframe in frame 25

For the outlander text layer.

11 Drag the **Outlander Spices** text to the end of the guide path

Grab the text block by the Spices text and try to position the end of the guide path in the center of the circle, as shown.

12 Create a motion tween between frames 10 and 25

(For the outlander text layer.) Right-click anywhere between frames 10 and 25 and choose Create Motion Tween.

13 Drag the playhead between frames 10 and 25

The text moves along the guide path. You will continue to make changes to the animation.

Hide the guide layer

(Click the dot in the Eye column on the Timeline.) You'll most likely want to hide any guide layer you draw after you're finished with it.

14 Save your changes

Motion tween speed

From the Property inspector, you can apply an Ease effect to your motion tweened animations. To ease a motion tween is to control the acceleration or deceleration in an object's movement. A positive Ease value makes an object accelerate quickly at the beginning and then decelerate at the end of its motion. A negative value produces the opposite effect.

To control the speed of a motion tween:

1 Select any keyframe within the motion tween.
2 On the Property inspector, enter a value in the Ease box.
3 Play the animation to view the results.
4 Change the value in the Ease box as needed.

C-4: Controlling the speed of a motion tween

Here's how	Here's why
1 Select frame 10	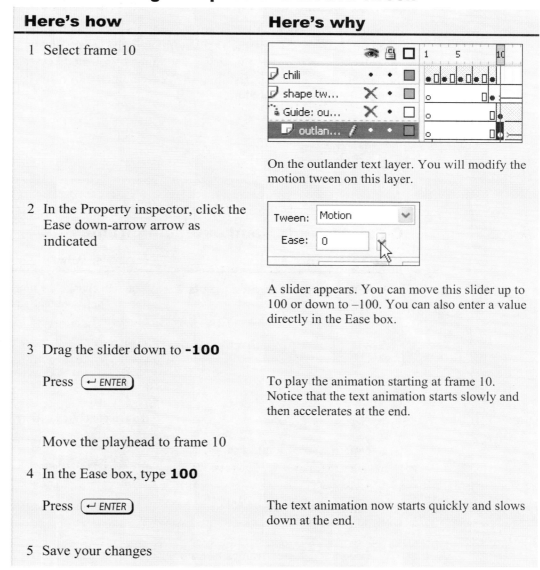
	On the outlander text layer. You will modify the motion tween on this layer.
2 In the Property inspector, click the Ease down-arrow arrow as indicated	
	A slider appears. You can move this slider up to 100 or down to –100. You can also enter a value directly in the Ease box.
3 Drag the slider down to **-100**	
Press (↵ ENTER)	To play the animation starting at frame 10. Notice that the text animation starts slowly and then accelerates at the end.
Move the playhead to frame 10	
4 In the Ease box, type **100**	
Press (↵ ENTER)	The text animation now starts quickly and slows down at the end.
5 Save your changes	

Arrange and extend frames

Explanation

The order in which you arrange and extend frames on the Timeline is critical to any animation. You can easily move keyframes around on the Timeline so that the content in a given layer appears at the desired moment in time. You can also extend the length of a keyframe so that content remains on the Stage for a longer period of time. Likewise, you can delete a frame or series of frames to reduce the duration that that content appears on the Stage.

To extend a frame, which extends its duration along the Timeline, you simply need to insert new frames within a keyframe. To do this, select the keyframe and choose Insert, Timeline, Frame, or press F5. If you want to extend the duration of multiple layers at once, press and hold the Ctrl key and click to select a desired frame for those layers, or use the Shift key and select the frame for layers in a sequential range, and then choose Insert, Timeline, Keyframe.

Selecting multiple keyframes

If you need to move multiple keyframes at once, you can use the Shift key to select a range of keyframes. Click the first keyframe in the series, and hold the Shift key. Then, click the last keyframe in the series. The range of selected keyframes appears black on the Timeline, as shown in Exhibit 6-8. You can then move this entire selection to a desired frame on the Timeline.

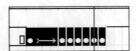

Exhibit 6-8: A range of selected keyframes

Do it!

C-5: Arranging and extending frames

Here's how	Here's why
1 Select the first frame on the black line layer	You will change the time in which this layer appears in the animation by moving its keyframes.
Press (SHIFT) and click frame 10	![outlander..., black line, right red ... layers] To select all the keyframes on this layer.
Drag the selection to frame 14	![outlander..., black line, right red ... layers]
2 Select all the frames on the chili layer	(The top layer on the Timeline.) Use the Shift key.
Drag the selected frames to frame 32	

3 Select all the frames on the shape
   tween layer

   Drag the selected frames to frame
   32

4 Select frame 60 on the black line   Click to select it.
   layer

   Press (SHIFT)

   Select frame 60 on the left red box   (The last layer in the Timeline.) To select frame
   layer   60 for all three layers.

   Choose **Insert**, **Timeline**,
   Keyframe

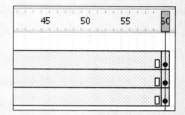

   To insert a keyframe at frame 60 for all three
   layers. This extends the duration of the
   animation to 60 frames and extends the time that
   the content of these layers appears on the Stage.

5 Insert a keyframe at frame 60 for   To extend the length of time for which this layer
   the outlander text layer   appears on the Stage.

6 From the Zoom list, select
   Show Frame

7 Press (⏎ ENTER)   To play the movie.

8 Save your changes and close the
   file

Unit summary: Animation

Topic A In this topic, you learned how to create a basic **text animation**. You learned about the components of the **Timeline** and how to use it. You also learned about **frames** and **keyframes**, and you learned how to play a movie in the work area to test your results as you work.

Topic B In this topic, you learned about **frame-by-frame** and **tweened** animations. You also learned how to convert a graphic into a symbol so that you can reuse instances of that symbol multiple times without adding file size to the movie. You also learned how to view and use the **Library**. Then, you learned how to edit **symbol instances**, and use **Onion Skin** to help you modify a frame-by-frame animation.

Topic C In this topic, you learned how to create a **shape tweened** and a **motion tweened** animation. You learned how to use **shape hints** to control a shape tween. You also learned how to use the arrow keys to precisely move objects on the Stage, and you learned how to use a **motion guide** and draw a **guide path**. Then, you learned how to control an animation's speed by using the **Ease control**, and you learned how to arrange and extend frames on the Timeline to create desired animation effects.

Independent practice activity

1 Open Animation practice.

2 Save the file as **My animation practice** in the current unit folder.

3 Insert a keyframe on frame 50 of the chili layer.

4 Give the chili image a width of **380** and a height of **200**. (*Hint*: Select the chili on the Stage at frame 50, and adjust the W and H settings on the Property inspector.)

5 Position the chili image so that it's centered over the text, as shown in Exhibit 6-9.

6 Create a motion tween between frames 40 and 50 on the chili layer.

7 Bring the playhead back to frame 1, and press Enter to play the movie and view your changes.

8 Make another modification of your choice, and play the movie.

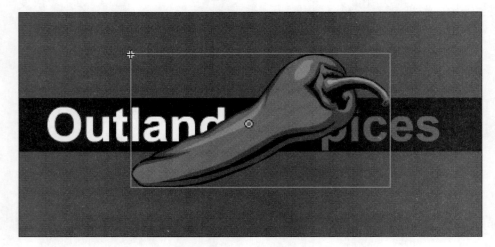

Exhibit 6-9: The enlarged chili image centered over the text

Unit 7

Button symbols

Unit time: 30 minutes

Complete this unit, and you'll know how to:

A Create and edit button symbols, and duplicate and swap buttons.

Topic A: Button symbols

Explanation

You can convert a text block, graphic, or grouped object into a button symbol. A button symbol is similar to a graphic symbol, although button symbols can be interactive.

Editing buttons and button states

Mouse events are actions that are triggered when a button is clicked or the pointer is moved over a button. For example, clicking a link or a form's Submit button triggers an event. Button symbols have four states: Up, Over, Down, and Hit. These states refer to the state of the button when a user takes a particular action to trigger the state. The following table describes each state.

State	Description
Up	The default, or initial, state of the button at the beginning of the movie or when no mouse event takes place
Over	This state is triggered when the mouse pointer is placed over the button
Down	This state is triggered when the mouse button is being clicked
Hit	Shows the defined area that responds to a mouse event; you can draw a shape to define the size of a button's Hit area

To incorporate these states into a button symbol, Flash creates a Timeline specific to the button symbol, as shown in Exhibit 7-1.

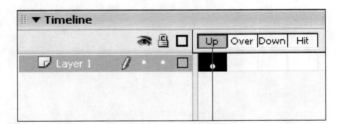

Exhibit 7-1: The Timeline for a button symbol in symbol editing mode

To create a button symbol, choose Insert, New Symbol and specify Button as the symbol type. To convert an existing image into a button symbol, select the image and choose Modify, Convert to Symbol. In the Convert to Symbol dialog box, select Button, and then set the button's *registration point*, which is the reference point for modifications such as rotation, movement, and scaling.

Editing button symbols

You can change the properties of a button symbol, such as its size, color, and alpha. To edit a button symbol, you can double-click the symbol. This is equivalent to right-clicking the symbol and selecting Edit in Place. This editing mode makes all other content on the Stage dimmed, allowing you to modify only that symbol. It also displays the button's own Timeline. You can also right-click the symbol and choose Edit. This displays the button on a new Stage area. Any changes that you make in symbol-editing mode affect all instances of that symbol.

Above the Timeline, you'll see that Flash provides a simple way to navigate between the symbol editing mode and the Flash document (Scene 1), as shown in Exhibit 7-2.

Exhibit 7-2: A document in symbol-editing mode

Testing button symbols

You can test the changes you make to your button symbols right in the document window by choosing Control, Enable Simple Buttons. When this option is enabled and you point to your finished button symbols, you will see your button states in action. To disable the option and continue working, choose Control, Enable Simple Buttons again.

Do it!

A-1:   Creating and editing a button symbol

Here's how	Here's why
1 Open Button symbols.fla	(From the current unit folder.) You will modify the navigation buttons in this document.
From the Zoom list, select **100%**	If necessary.
2 Save the file as **My Button symbols**	In the current unit folder.
3 Select **Locations**	
	(Use the Selection tool.) Scroll up in the document to select Locations.
Observe the Property inspector	
	This object is a group of two separate shapes. You'll convert it to a button symbol and then break it apart to access its individual components.
4 Right-click **Locations** and choose **Convert to Symbol...**	To open the Convert to Symbol dialog box.
5 In the Name box, enter **locationsButton**	
Select **Button**	
Set the Registration point to the center, as shown	
Click **OK**	

6 Observe the Locations button

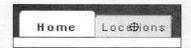

A circle with a plus sign appears in the center of the button. The position of the plus sign corresponds to the position of the registration point you set.

Observe the Property inspector

It now displays options for modifying a button symbol.

Open the Library panel

(If necessary.) Press Ctrl+L.

7 In the Library panel, double-click the **locationsButton** icon

(Move the Library panel to see the button on the stage.) The symbol appears alone on the Stage, in symbol-editing mode. Notice that a whole new Timeline appears. You'll specify the behavior of the button in the Up, Over, Down, and Hit states.

Observe the Timeline

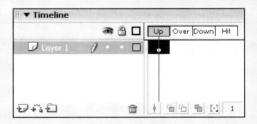

There are four possible states that you can apply to the locationsButton symbol.

Observe the area above the Timeline

Flash provides an easy way to navigate between the document (Scene 1) and the component you're editing.

8   From the Zoom list, select **200%**

9   Choose **Modify**, **Break Apart**

To break apart the locationsButton symbol so that you can modify its separate shapes. The button is broken into a tab area and a text label.

Click anywhere in the white area

To deselect the shapes.

On the Timeline, right-click as shown

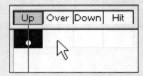

To display a shortcut menu.

Choose **Insert Keyframe**

To insert a keyframe for the Over state.

Click anywhere in the white background

To deselect the shapes.

10   Click the background region, as shown

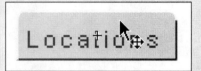

You'll change this color for the Over stage of the button.

On the Property inspector, change the fill color to **FFEFDF**

(Click the Fill Color box and enter FFEFDF in the value box.) This will be the tab's color in the Over state when the pointer is placed over the button.

Deselect the **Locations** button

Click any area around the Locations button.

11   Insert a keyframe in the Down state

Double-click the text **Locations**

The text appears in text editing mode, and the Text tool is automatically selected.

Select the text

Make the text bold

On the Property inspector, click the Bold button.

12 Click **Scene 1**

To leave symbol-editing mode and return to the document.

13 In the Library panel, click **locationsButton**

A preview of the button appears in the Preview pane.

Click the play button, as indicated

The color and font style changes are shown, as they will in the Over state and Down state.

14 Choose **Control**, **Enable Simple Buttons**

To show the behavior of the button in each state.

Point to the **Locations** button

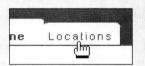

The background color changes according to the color you specified for the Over state.

Click the button

The text becomes bold in the Down state.

15 Choose **Control**, **Enable Simple Buttons**

To disable button testing in the document.

Save your changes

Duplicating and swapping symbols

Explanation

You can easily duplicate a symbol if you want to create similar symbols. Duplicating symbols saves time if you need to create several similar symbols and use them repeatedly. For example, if you want to create navigation buttons, such as Next and Previous buttons, you can create one button, make it a symbol, and then duplicate the symbol and then change its text content to create a new button.

You can use any of the following methods to duplicate a symbol:

- On the Stage, right-click the symbol and choose Duplicate Symbol. Enter the name in the Duplicate Symbol dialog box, and click OK.

- In the Library, right-click the symbol and choose Duplicate. Enter the name in the Duplicate Symbol dialog box, and click OK.

- From the Library, drag the symbol to the Stage, right-click the new instance, and select Duplicate Symbol. Enter the name in the Duplicate Symbol dialog box, and click OK.

Swapping symbols

If you want to change the order in which your buttons appear, or replace one with another, you can easily swap them by using the Swap button. You can use either of the following methods to swap a symbol:

- On the Stage, right-click the symbol and choose Swap Symbol to open the Swap Symbol dialog box. Choose the symbol that will replace the one selected on the Stage, and click OK.

- On the Stage, select the symbol and choose Modify, Symbol, Swap Symbol to open the Swap Symbol dialog box. Choose the symbol that will replace the one selected on the Stage, and click OK.

Do it!

A-2: Duplicating and swapping a button

Here's how	Here's why
1 In the Library, select **locationsButton**	
Drag the symbol from the Library to the indicated position	
	To create a new instance of this button symbol.
2 Observe the Property inspector	
	Instance of: locationsButton
	This is a new instance of the locationsButton symbol.
3 Right-click the new button	
Choose **Duplicate Symbol...**	To open the Duplicate Symbol dialog box.
4 Edit the Symbol name to read **AboutUsButton**	
	Duplicate Symbol
	Symbol name: AboutUsButton OK / Cancel
Click **OK**	
5 Observe the Property inspector	
	Instance of: AboutUsButton
	The new button is now an instance of the AboutUsButton symbol.
Observe the Library panel	The Library panel contains the new AboutUsButton symbol.
6 In the Library, double-click the **AboutUsButton** icon	You'll edit the text in this symbol.
Double-click the button symbol	On the Stage.
Edit the text to read **About Us**	About Us

7 Edit the text for the Over and Down states to read **About Us**

In the Timeline panel, select each button state, and then change the text in each state.

Click **Scene 1**

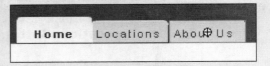

The About Us button is updated.

8 Select the **Locations** button

(Use the Selection tool.) You'll swap the Locations button with the About Us button.

Click **Swap**

(In the Property inspector.) To open the Swap Symbol dialog box.

9 Click **AboutUsButton**

Click **OK**

The Locations button is swapped with the About Us button.

10 Select the second About Us button

You'll swap this About Us button with the Locations button.

Open the Swap Symbol dialog box

Select **locationsButton**

Click **OK**

11 Observe the buttons

The About Us button is swapped with the Locations button.

12 Choose **Control, Enable Simple Buttons**

Test the Over and Down states for both buttons

Save your changes and close the file

Unit summary: Button symbols

Topic A

In this topic, you learned how to create and edit **button symbols**. You learned how to customize and test **button states**. Finally, you learned how to duplicate and swap button symbols.

Independent practice activity

1 Open Practice buttons.fla.

2 Save the file as **My practice buttons** in the current unit folder.

3 Create two new buttons named **Products** and **Order**, and place them on the navigation bar, as shown in Exhibit 7-3.

4 Center the text Products and Order on their buttons.

5 Test the buttons to make sure they all behave the same way. (*Hint*: Choose Control, Enable Simple Buttons.)

6 Save your changes and close the file.

Exhibit 7-3: The completed navigation bar

Flash MX 2004: Basic

Course summary

This summary contains information to help
you bring the course to a successful
conclusion. Using this information, you will
be able to:

A Use the summary text to reinforce what
you've learned in class.

B Determine the next courses in this series
(if any), as well as any other resources that
might help you continue to learn about
Flash MX 2004.

Topic A: Course summary

Use the following summary text to reinforce what you've learned in class.

Flash MX 2004: Basic

Unit 1

In this unit, you learned about the components of the Flash environment, and how to create and save a new Flash file. You also learned how to specify a document's **dimensions** and **background color**. Then, you learned the difference between **raster** and **vector** graphics, and you learned how to import and manipulate images. Then, you learned how to use the **Free Transform** tool and its **modifiers**, and how to convert a bitmap (raster) image to a vector image. Then you learned how to create lines and curves by using the Pencil and Pen tools. Finally, you learned how to use rulers and apply basic **line styles**.

Unit 2

In this unit, you learned how to create basic shapes, such as rectangles, squares, ovals and circles by using the Rectangle and Oval tools. You also learned how to create **freeform shapes**. Then, you learned how to use the Selection, Subselection, and Lasso tools, how to change line styles, **transform shapes**, and copy, move and delete a shape. Finally, you learned how to **group** shapes.

Unit 3

In this unit, you learned how to use the **Fill Color** and **Stroke Color** boxes. You also learned how to use the Paint Bucket and Ink Bottle tools to apply fill and stroke colors. Then, you learned how to copy an existing color for re-use in a document, and apply different **brush styles**. Finally, you learned how to use the **Color Mixer** to create and save a **custom color**, create **linear** and **radial gradients**, customize gradient colors, and save a custom gradient.

Unit 4

In this unit, you learned how to create **extending text blocks** and **fixed text blocks**. You learned how to move and resize text blocks. Then, you learned how to use the **Property Inspector** to change the font face, font size, and color of text. Then, you learned how to use the Property Inspector to create bold and italic text. Then, you learned how to **skew**, **scale**, and **align text**, and create **aliased** text. You then learned how to adjust text spacing, and how to apply **margins** and **indentation**. Finally, you learned how use the Find and Replace feature, the Spell Checker, and the **History panel**.

Unit 5

In this unit, you learned how to work with **layers**. You also learned how to **create** a **new layer**, **rearrange** and **merge** layers, and **delete** a layer. Then, you learned how to modify layers, name layers, and lock layers to prevent them from being modified. Then, you learned how to **hide** a layer and **mask** a layer to display only specific portions of a layer or the layers below that layer. Finally, you learned how to organize layers by creating folders, and you learned how to create a **guide layer**.

Unit 6

In this unit, you learned how to create a basic **text animation**. You learned about the components of the **Timeline** and how to use it. You also learned about **frames** and **keyframes**, and you learned how play a movie in the work area to test your results. Then, you learned about **frame-by-frame** and **tweened animations**. You learned how to convert a graphic into a **symbol**, and how to view and use the **Library**. Then, you learned how to edit symbols, and use **Onion Skin** to help you modify a frame-by-frame animation. Then, you learned how to create a **shape tweened** and a **motion tweened animation**. You learned how to use **shape hints** and **motion guides**, and you learned how to control an animation's speed by using the **Ease control**. Finally, you learned how to arrange and extend frames on the Timeline to create desired animation effects.

Unit 7

In this topic, you learned how to create and edit **button symbols**. You learned how to customize and test **button states**. Finally, you learned how to duplicate and swap button symbols.

Topic B: Continued learning after class

It is impossible to learn to use any software effectively in a single day. To get the most out of this class, you should begin working with Flash MX 2004 to perform real tasks as soon as possible. Course Technology also offers resources for continued learning.

Next courses in this series

This is the first course in this series. The next course in this series is:

- *Flash MX 2004: Advanced*

Flash MX 2004: Basic

Quick reference

Button	Shortcut keys	Function
🔍	Z or M	Magnifies shapes or images
✋	H	Used to scroll within a document
▲	V	Selects or moves an object
▲	A	Displays and selects points on a path or objects in a group
✏️	Y	Draws freehand lines with the current stroke color
🖌️	B	Adds brush-like strokes to an image
／	N	Draws straight lines
▢	R	Draws a rectangle or square
⊡	Q	Transforms images, instances, or text blocks
○	O	Draws an oval or circle
✒️	P	Draws straight and curved paths
◗	L	Draws a freeform selection
▱	E	Erases unwanted parts of a shape
🪣	K	Changes the fill color of a shape

Button	Shortcut keys	Function
A	⌴T⌴	Inserts a text block
	⌴F⌴	Transforms a gradient or bitmap fill
	⌴S⌴	Applies a stroke color to a shape
	⌴I⌴	Copies the stroke or fill color of a shape

Index